Susan Jeffers Ph.D. is an internationally renowned author who has helped millions of people overcome their fears and heal the pain in their lives. She is also a public speaker, workshop leader and media personality who specializes in the areas of personal growth and relationships. She lives with her husband in Los Angeles.

FEEL THE FEAR
... AND BEYOND

DYNAMIC TECHNIQUES FOR
Doing It Anyway

SUSAN JEFFERS

Vermilion
LONDON

Copyright© Susan Jeffers 1998

Susan Jeffers has asserted her right to be identified as the Author of this work in accordance with the Copyright, Designs and Patents Act, 1988

First published in 1998 in Great Britain by Rider, an imprint of Ebury Press, Random House. 20 Vauxhall Bridge Road, London SW1V 2SA www.randomhouse.co.uk This edition published in 2000

Addresses for companies within The Random House Group Limited can be found at: www.randomhouse.co.uk

The Random House Group Limited Reg. No. 954009

Typeset by SX Composing DTP, Rayleigh, Essex

A CIP catalogue record for this book is available from the British Library

ISBN 9780712608831

Penguin Random House is committed to a sustainable future for our business, our readers and our planet. This book is made from Forest Stewardship Council® certified paper.

MIX
Paper from
responsible sources
FSC
www.fsc.org FSC® C018179

Printed and bound in Great Britain by Clays Ltd, St Ives plc

To the many people
who have let me know I've
made a difference in
their lives.

Please know that you've truly
made a difference in mine.

My deepest thanks.

ACKNOWLEDGEMENTS

A big thank you to my editor, Judith Kendra, who encouraged me to write this book . . . and to all the people at Random House who lovingly made it a reality.

A big thank you to my American agent, Dominick Abel, and my British agent, David Grossman, who have always had my best interests at heart. As a bonus, I've loved the lunches and dinners and laughs we've shared over the years.

A big thank you to my daughter, Leslie Gershman, who contributed her valuable insights about many aspects of this book. She lives her life in a 'Do It Anyway' fashion and it's wonderful to watch.

And, as always, a big kiss, a hug and thank you to my wonderful husband, Mark Shelmerdine, who never lets a day go by without letting me know, in words and actions, how much he loves me. My darling Mark, the feeling is mutual.

CONTENTS

PART I

Introduction

One of the most fulfilling experiences of my life has been the success of *Feel the Fear and Do It Anyway*. It is now available in twenty-three countries and as letters come in from thankful readers near and far, I am filled with a deep sense of gratitude. I am so happy we have touched each other's lives.

In a way, *Feel the Fear . . . and Beyond* is a 'thank you' to the many friends I've made throughout the world. It is my response to those who have asked me to create a companion book to help make the exercises in *Feel the Fear and Do It Anyway* become a meaningful part of their everyday lives. It's one thing to know what these exercises are; it's another to take this knowing deep within your being so that you have the courage to live your life as you would like to live it. And that requires the kind of practice this book offers.

In addition to the exercises that are included, I've interspersed some very moving letters I've received from people who have made dramatic alterations to the way they see the world as a result of doing the exercises. Hopefully the reading of these letters will keep your commitment strong. While I've naturally changed them a little to protect the identity of the writers, the essence of the letters demonstrates the power that the exercises have to transport you to the best of who you are and make you powerful in the face of your fears.

I remember a time many years ago when I was paralysed with fear. The world out there seemed vast and scary. Now the world seems to have shrunk to a very manageable size . . . and I love being in it. I can tell you that my ability to keep moving forward with my life, despite any fear I encounter along the way, is a result of my commitment to practise the exercises I learned from my many teachers over the years.

I ask you to make this same commitment. Trust me when I tell you that the negativity in the world will always try to pull you down and make you weak. It is up to you to take an active role in remaining powerful and loving *despite what is happening in the outside world*. As you commit to doing the exercises, slowly you begin to 'live into' the part of you that is filled with courage, trust, love, fulfilment, joy and all good things. The yearning disappears. You will have found the best of who you are. *It doesn't get any better than that.*

I have M.E. (myalgia encephalomyelitis). I work as a consultant for a large firm. I contracted the disease a year ago and have been off work ever since. I have muscle problems and suffer from general lethargy. Recently I became deeply depressed about my situation; my inability to play with my wonderful child, my limitless anger and frustration, my perceived hopelessness of my condition, the threat of redundancy, my drift into anti-social behaviour (this list could take at least another page!)

I went away for a couple of days on my own in order to clarify the whirlpool of thoughts I had washing around my tortured mind. When I returned I felt as though I were beginning on a path out of my morass but I didn't really know what to do or how to do it. Then by complete good fortune I happened upon a copy of your fantastic book Feel the Fear and Do It Anyway. The ideas you present in it are so simple, logical and inspiring that I immediately began to carry out the exercises.

That was one month ago. My doctors, family and friends are amazed at the change in my outlook. My life force and spirit, which I always had in abundance before my illness, are back and are helping me through the most difficult aspects of my condition.

I cannot thank you enough for touching my life in such a practical and profound way. I still have bad days, but learn from them now instead of wallowing in them. I am not yet physically well enough to return to work, but I believe that I will completely recover in time to save my job. I am not even that worried if I do lose my job, because I now know that whatever happens will bring its own opportunities and rewards.

Thank you . . .
T. F.
Salisbury, UK

PART II

Reminders from 'The Source'

I f it's been some time since you read *Feel the Fear and Do It Anyway*, it is a good idea to re-visit it now. If you haven't read it (horrors!) I suggest you do. Since the enclosed exercises are based on the principles in *Feel the Fear and Do It Anyway*, reading it will enrich your experience of this particular book enormously. (I've provided endnotes to direct you to relevant sections.) Also, please read the following reminders frequently. They are meant to help you remember why it is so important to master the tools I am presenting. It is so easy to forget!

REMINDERS

What Are We Afraid Of? All of us can name many situations that keep us in a state of fear. For example, fear of ageing, rejection, ending a relationship, losing a loved one, not having enough money, becoming ill, and on and on and on. This is a good time for you to think about the fears you encounter in all areas of your life. And as they come into your mind, write them in the following space. (As with all the exercises in this book, really take the time to think about your responses.)

The fears that run my life are:

....

....

....

....

I suspect that all the fears you've listed above are what I call 'surface' fears. They apply to situations regarding career, relationships, money, health, ageing, acceptance, loss and the like. I call them surface fears because they only scratch the surface. If you look a little deeper you find the BIG fear . . . the *real* fear which is the underlying cause of all your other fears. And what is that fear? It is the fear that you won't be able to handle whatever life brings you!

If you knew that you could handle anything that came your way, what would you possibly have to fear? Nothing!

The exercises in this book go a long way in helping you create the confidence that you *can* handle whatever life brings you in a powerful and loving way.

WHAT A GREAT REASON TO DO THE EXERCISES!

Why Do We Grow Up Having So Little Confidence in our Ability to Handle Whatever Happens in our Lives? Well, it could be our conditioning. I love to point out that in all my years, I have never heard a parent calling out to a child going off to school: 'Take some risks today, darling . . .' On the contrary, the words we hear are usually: 'Be careful . . .' Ultimately, it's a wonder we have the courage to walk out the door!

But we are not here to blame our parents. (Nor am I suggesting we tell our children to put themselves in physically dangerous situations!) Blame is a powerless act. There is no need to blame anyone or anything for who we are at this moment in time. Instead we pick up the tools which are embodied in this book to help us build our courage in the here and now.

WHAT A GREAT REASON TO DO THE EXERCISES!

Why Do These Exercises Work? They work because they teach us how to access the greatest resource within our being: the 'Higher Self'. The Higher Self is the space within each and every one of us that is filled with all nourishing qualities such as joy, creativity, intuition, peace, power, love, compassion and all good things.

I'm sure there have been moments, however fleeting, when you have been able to access this transcendent place within. At those times, all seemed right with the world. The fear and struggle were replaced by a sense that '*All is well*', but the feeling never lasts. Why? Because it is our tendency to revert to a more familiar part of ourselves which I call the 'Lower Self'.

You'll recognize the Lower Self as the place within that is filled with all negative qualities such as anger, judgement, a sense of scarcity, helplessness and, of course, fear. If you want to live a joyful and creative life, therefore, your task seems very clear . . . and that is to *become a Higher-Self thinker instead of a Lower-Self thinker*. Each of the exercises in this book is meant to help you accomplish this goal.

WHAT A GREAT REASON TO DO THE EXERCISES!

Why Do We Hang On to Lower-Self Living When It Is So Negative? I believe that Lower-Self living is a habit. Habit is defined as an acquired pattern of behaviour that has become *involuntary* as a result of frequent repetition. We now have to make Higher-Self living a habit. Wouldn't it be wonderful if we involuntarily thought in a loving and powerful way? Indeed!

So how do we break undesirable old habits? *Through constant repetition of the desired behaviour*. The exercises provide constant repetition of desired behaviour and, therefore, are the habit breakers we need. Ultimately they allow us to think in a Higher-Self way. They engage the Spirit. They awaken us to a beautiful way of seeing the world around us.

WHAT A GREAT REASON TO DO THE EXERCISES!

When We Do These Exercises, Does the Fear Go Away? In *Feel the Fear and Do It Anyway*, I introduced you to a number of 'truths' about fear. Fear Truth 1 is very telling:

FEAR TRUTH 1: THE FEAR WILL NEVER GO AWAY AS LONG AS YOU CONTINUE TO GROW!

Every time you take a step into the unknown, you experience fear. There is no point in saying, 'When I am no longer afraid, then I will do it.' You'll be waiting a long time! The fear is part of the package. The exercises help you to move forward despite the fear. They help you '*do it anyway*'. They give you courage. They allow you to see things in a new and powerful way.

WHAT A GREAT REASON TO DO THE EXERCISES!

What Are the Other Truths about Fear? The other truths about fear offer some interesting insights as well. They are:

FEAR TRUTH 2: THE ONLY WAY TO GET RID OF THE

FEAR OF DOING SOMETHING IS TO GO OUT . . . AND DO IT!

When you 'do it' often enough, you will no longer be afraid in that particular situation. You will have faced the unknown and you will have handled it. Then new challenges await you . . . which certainly adds to the excitement in living!

FEAR TRUTH 3: THE ONLY WAY TO FEEL BETTER ABOUT YOURSELF IS TO GO OUT . . . AND DO IT!

With each little step you take into unknown territory, a pattern of strength develops. You begin feeling stronger and stronger and stronger.

FEAR TRUTH 4: NOT ONLY ARE YOU GOING TO EXPERIENCE FEAR WHENEVER YOU'RE ON UN-FAMILIAR TERRITORY, BUT SO IS EVERYONE ELSE!

This should be a relief! You're not the only one out there feeling fear. *Everyone feels fear when taking a step into the unknown.* Yes, all those people out there who have succeeded in doing what they have wanted to do in life have felt the fear . . . and did it anyway! So can you.

FEAR TRUTH 5: PUSHING THROUGH FEAR IS LESS FRIGHTENING THAN LIVING WITH THE UNDER-LYING FEAR THAT COMES FROM A FEELING OF HELPLESSNESS!

This is the one that some people have trouble understanding. Trust me when I tell you that as you push through the fear, you will feel such a sense of relief as your feeling of helplessness subsides. You will wonder why you didn't take action sooner. You will become more and more aware that you truly *can* handle anything that life brings you.

As you look at these truths about fear, particularly Truth 4, you see that FEAR IS NOT THE PROBLEM. If fear were the problem, *nobody* would be moving forward with their lives. No, fear is not the problem; it is how we *hold* that fear. Do we hold it from a position of pain, paralysis and depression (the position of the Lower Self) or a position of power, action and love (the position of the Higher Self)? Obviously, our task is very clear. It is to move ourselves from a position of pain about fear to one of power. And, once again, that is the purpose of the exercises.

WHAT A GREAT REASON TO DO THE EXERCISES!

How Long Do We Have to Do the Exercises? For a lifetime! Sorry about that! I don't know why we can't just become powerful and stay that way. What I do know is that if we don't exercise the muscle that takes us to the Highest part of who we are, it weakens and we begin to fall back into a state of pain and paralysis once again. We become asleep to the power and love that lie within.

I liken it to our physical bodies. We must *use* the muscles in our body to keep in great physical shape, that is, we must exercise. In the same way, we must *use* the muscles that take us to our Higher Self, that is, we must exercise! That's just the way it is.

WHAT A GREAT REASON TO DO THE EXERCISES!

Why Haven't I Known about the Higher Self Before? I see the Higher Self as the spiritual part of who we are. Our society talks of Body, Mind and Spirit. Yet the emphasis is almost totally on Body and Mind (and I might add money!) Little is taught about the spiritual part of who we are. Even religion often alienates us from our powerful and loving natures, for example, when it asks us to judge or to exclude others. As a result, we are seldom in touch with the part of us that is loving, joyful, creative, intuitive, powerful and knows there is nothing to fear.

Instead of Higher-Self living, we are taught Lower-Self living by a very fearful society. Just listening to the news can put terror in our hearts! We learn to hear only the voice of doom and gloom . . . the voice that is fearful, judgemental, angry, insecure and all negative things.

But, again, we can't blame society! We can't blame anyone or anything. Blame makes us victims. And feeling like a victim is the most frightening place in which to be! We need to take responsibility for rising above the world of the Lower Self and finding our way to the Higher Self . . . despite the negative teachings of our society. In that way, we can heal our lives . . . and make it a better world for everyone around us.

WHAT A GREAT REASON TO DO THE EXERCISES!

How Do I Know If I Am in the Land of the Lower Self or the Higher Self? Oh, that's easy. If your mind is generally filled with messages of lack, scarcity, anger, jealousy, judgement, fear and any form of negativity, you can be sure you are in the land of the Lower Self. If you generally hear messages of creativity, abundance, compassion, courage, joy and any form of power and love, you are in the land of the Higher Self.

I have named the voice of the Lower Self the 'Chatterbox'. A friend of mine named his Stanley! Later you'll have a chance to name yours. You might be wondering, 'Susan, what voice are you talking about?' It is the inner voice of gloom and doom that doesn't let you see anything in a positive way. If you stop and listen to it right now, you probably won't hear it but when you are feeling upset about something in your life, just take a moment to listen. It is the voice that is telling you:

> You aren't pretty (or handsome) enough;
> You won't get the job you want;
> You said the wrong thing at an interview;
> You don't have what it takes to succeed;
> Your dinner party wasn't good enough;
> You can't survive without your mate.

Of course, once you become aware of the Chatterbox, you'll hate me because you won't be able to turn it off! At least not for a while! I promise that as you do the exercises, the messages of the Higher Self will become more dominant in your thinking and the Chatterbox will thankfully lose its power to run (and ruin) your life!

WHAT A GREAT REASON TO DO THE EXERCISES!

You Talk about the Higher Self. Where Does God Fit in All of This? Wherever is appropriate for you. There are those who do not believe in God or a Higher Power. In this case, their Higher Selves can provide a huge amount of inner strength. I've known some people who have had a great sense of self and purpose in this world and who have done wonderful things, yet did not believe in God. Their conscious or unconscious connection with their Higher Selves sustained them through difficult times.

On the other hand, there are those who do believe in God, a Higher Power, the Force, or whatever it may be for you. I am one of them. In recent years particularly, I constantly feel a Divine presence in my life. And my Higher Self is my connection to that Divine Presence. I have learned that with a deep trust in my Higher Self *plus* a deep trust in my Higher Power, my fear doesn't have a chance to hold me back. This is true for you as well.

It stands to reason that when we are feeling fearful, we have lost our connection to one or both of these incredible sources of power. It is at such times that we need to pick up one of the exercises described in this book and reconnect once again . . . and what a grand feeling that is!

WHAT A GREAT REASON TO DO THE EXERCISES!

By now you've got the point. The use of spiritual exercises, such as the ones enclosed in this book, is very important. It becomes a matter of asking yourself:

'Do I really want to go through life feeling afraid and missing out on so much of the beauty that life has to offer? Or do I want to take the steps that bring me to a place of trust, power, fulfilment and love?'

One would have to be seriously in need of psychological help to choose the former!

Let me end this section with another wonderful reason to do the exercises. There is nothing as satisfying as taking ACTION. Action in itself is very powerful. It helps us sculpt our experience of life, instead of feeling we have no choices. Indeed, we do have many choices. And doing everything we can to transport ourselves to the realm of the Higher Self is absolutely the very best choice we can make.

WHAT A GREAT REASON TO DO THE EXERCISES!

I am not a person who is 'stuck'. I go after what I want. However, the fear I feel takes away my confidence and takes me away from the feeling of adventure. You reminded me that I am not alone in my fear; that awareness itself greatly reduces the impact of fear.

P. N.
Chicago, USA

PART III

How to Use This Book

ON YOUR OWN

F eel the Fear . . . and Beyond is really a 'discovery book' filled with explanations and exercises that are insightful, comical, rewarding and, ultimately, life-changing. Every time you get involved and take part in the activities, you are moving further and further toward your goal of pushing through fear.

While I give you suggestions about how to use each of the exercises, there are no rigid rules. In fact, if you can think how to alter them in a way more suited to your life-style, that's great! Many of my students have come up with very inventive uses for the exercises, thus increasing their fun and effectiveness in using them. So be as creative as you want to be. What is not wise is to read this book then sit down for an afternoon and rattle through the exercises, saying to your-self, 'Fine, I've got that!' Instead, I would suggest you spend at least twenty minutes a day or more using the exercises. Remember:

CONSTANT REPETITION OF DESIRABLE THOUGHTS AND BEHAVIOUR IS THE KEY TO CHANGING UN-DESIRABLE THOUGHTS AND BEHAVIOUR.

If you are very busy, not to worry. Most of these exercises can be used during the course of everyday activities . . . while dressing, driving, working, taking care of the children and so on. In fact, *spiritual exercises are best practised when facing the challenges of everyday living.* Each new challenge offers us an opportunity to practise . . . practise . . . practise.

Keeping your goal in mind will help keep you focused and that goal, of course, is *to replace the voice of the Lower Self with the voice of the Higher Self*. Achieving this goal is an evolving process. For example, in the beginning you may repeat certain Higher-Self thoughts for twenty minutes a day. After a while, an appropriate Higher-Self thought will *automatically* insert itself when you are in the middle of thinking Lower-Self thoughts. It is then that you know you are making progress.

For example, if your Chatterbox is driving you crazy with troubling thoughts about the outcome of an event, you may hear another voice telling you, 'It's all happening perfectly. Not to worry!' And, for that moment in time, you feel a sense of peace. That voice, of course, is the voice of the confident and more powerful part of yourself: the Higher Self. As you continue to practise, slowly but surely, such healing thoughts will enter your consciousness more and more frequently. In this way you become powerful in the face of your fears.

Again, these tools are meant to be used for a lifetime. Every day of our lives can bring us difficult, frustrating, hurtful and scary experiences that can put us in the realm of discomfort and fear. You can imagine the fear I felt when I was told that I had breast cancer many years ago but, because I had my precious bag of spiritual tools, I was able to transform a potential tragedy into a triumph (see Chapter 3). No matter what life hands us, these spiritual tools are there to remind us that '*All is well*'.

Here, I have chosen a number of my favourite tools for building a 'fear-less' life. Notice that I am careful not to say a 'fearless' life. Fear Truth 1 tells us that by virtue of the fact that we are human, fear will always be a part of our lives as we learn and grow and step into the unknown – but we can learn to fear things less. The object is not to resist the fear but to 'do it anyway'. These are all 'do it anyway' tools.

To help you gauge your progress as you are doing the

exercises, it is helpful and fun to create for yourself a 'Pain-to-Power' chart, such as I have created below. Right now, pick a spot where you see yourself on the chart and mark it with a dot or oblique line or however you choose to mark it.

PAIN-TO-POWER CHART

PAIN   **POWER**

This is your starting point. As you do the exercises on a daily basis, you hopefully will see yourself moving closer and closer to the powerful part of who you are.

If you feel moved to do so, you can become very creative with your Pain-to-Power charts. Many of my students have created works of art which they have hung on their wall. Some have created different Pain-to-Power charts for different areas of their lives such as career, relationship, risk-taking and so on. You can have a lot of fun with this.

Also, in Section VI, I've created for you a '30-Day Power Planner' which includes a daily Pain-to-Power chart. Here you can keep a month's record of where you would place yourself after each day of practising your exercises.

Don't be upset if there are days when you seem to go backwards a bit. Life is like that! Unexpected situations often bring up a great deal of fear and may set us back a bit on our journey from pain to power. Not to worry! It is at such times that you know to intensify your use of the tools in this toolbox to remind yourself that, at the level of the Higher Self, 'ALL IS WELL!'

A word of warning: *Please, please, please, don't take this all too seriously.* Our Higher Self would definitely tell us to lighten up about life and have fun! One of my favourite sayings is, 'Angels fly because they take themselves lightly'. The Pain-to-Power chart and all the tools in this book need to be approached with a sense of curiosity, humour and adventure.

The most negative thing you can do is to berate yourself for not doing it right, or fast enough, or effectively enough or whatever else your Lower Self can conjure up to convince you that you are not good enough. *Just pat yourself on the back for every little step you take.* With enough practice, Higher-Self thinking will eventually dominate.

If, as you go through these exercises, you forget why you are doing them or you get lazy, go back to the reminders. They will help keep you on track. And, if you get lazy, ask yourself:

> 'Why would anyone choose to live in the land of the LOWER SELF when the land of the HIGHER SELF is ours for the taking?'

You might answer, 'Well, today, I *choose* to live in the land of the Lower Self! I'm going to enjoy every moment of my misery!' I've actually had days like that . . . and I've enjoyed every minute! Of course, my enjoyment came from the fact that I can choose to pull myself out of the misery. I am not a victim or a prisoner.

Commitment is the hard part. We somehow always start out with good intentions but then we 'forget' our commitment as our negative mind gets in the way. Does that sound familiar? To help keep your commitment strong, you may want to explore the idea of finding a 'buddy' for mutual encouragement. Daily phone calls – or messages left on the answerphone – reminding each other to do the exercises and focus on the positive will certainly help. Forming a group with other like-minded people to work through the exercises together also works beautifully (see the next section).

Also to help get you started with a strong sense of intention, the end of this chapter contains a commitment statement for you to sign. Sometimes our signature on a personal contract sets the tone for how we want to live our lives. Read the contract over slowly and thoughtfully. If you feel you are ready to sign it, then do so. If not, that's OK too. Perhaps in the working of the exercises, you will feel a sense of readiness that you are not feeling now. It will always be there for you to sign if you so choose.

Right now I commit to following the pathway to the best of who I am. I understand that this is a life-long commitment but with every step of the way I will be learning how to access the huge amount of power and love that I hold inside. I know that I may stray from the path at certain times in my life but I will always find my way back to this beautiful part of who I am.

....

Signature

....

Date

WITH A GROUP

love the idea of using this book as the basis of a self-help group. Now don't let the term 'group' frighten you. Participating in a group is not about airing your dirty laundry in public, as some people think. (It's amazing that we call normal human feelings 'dirty laundry', isn't it?) No, it's about like-minded people getting together on a regular basis and helping each other to learn, grow and to move forward in life with confidence and love.

There are many advantages to using this book in a group setting. For example, members encourage each other to stay committed to the exercises. Also, everyone breathes a sigh of relief when they realize that others experience the same fears and feelings of resistance that they do.

If you are unfamiliar with the group process, groups can range in size from three to hundreds of people. For the purpose of using this book as a basis for a self-help group, however, anywhere from three to ten people seems like a good size.

There are a number of decisions and actions to be taken as you get your group together:

1. *Decide whether you want the group to be single-sexed or mixed.* Each has distinct advantages but, in the end, the only thing that everyone needs to have in common is an interest in growing as a human being.

2. *Focus on enlisting a few people to join you.* Tell your friends. Tell your friends to tell their friends. Spread the word at work. Think about the activities in which you are involved.

I will wager many offer opportunities to enlist members. If you attend a workshop, make an announcement that you want to create a self-help group. In a few of the seminars I have given, such groups were created in just this way before the evening was over.

3. *Choose a meeting place.* This could be in an office or in the comfort of someone's home.

4. *Choose a time that works for everyone.* Some people like weekends. I like to make the group an evening activity including a very informal meal with each participant contributing some food. 'Breaking bread' is a great ice-breaker. It allows everyone to relax from the pressures of the day and helps them focus on the 'fear' exercises from about 7–9 or 10 pm.

5. *Decide how often you want to meet.* Weekly? Bi-weekly? Again, create what works for you.

6. *Agree to a finite number of meetings.* For the purposes of this book, a 14-week course of meetings is good. Use the first week to decide on the format and to choose which exercise everyone is to work on before the following session. Then, once all twelve exercises are completed, use the last week to discuss any progress individual members have made and their personal commitments for the future.

If the group members found the fourteen weeks a positive experience, they may choose to continue meeting indefinitely. I know some groups that have been meeting for over ten years. They use the exercises in my other books and other self-help titles that are available today, or they simply meet regularly to encourage each other to handle all situations in their lives in a Higher-Self way.

7. *Decide upon a format.* Here are a few suggestions. At the start of each meeting, you may want one of the members to read a statement of purpose such as the following:

'We have chosen to be here today for the purpose of reaching out and helping one another to grow into powerful and loving human beings. We commit to coming from that part of ourselves that is filled with integrity and caring. We commit to keeping what is said in this group confidential. We appreciate that we are all human beings doing the very best we can and that through our mutual compassion we can learn to see the light within us all.'[1]

Once the statement of purpose is shared, you may simply want to go around the room with each person describing their experience of the exercise of the week: what they noticed, felt and learned. You may be surprised to find how similar (or dissimilar) each member's experience was. Often this sharing helps you look at the exercise from many perspectives or helps you expand your thinking in a multitude of ways.

At the end of the meeting, it is wonderful for group members to thank each other for being there, preferably with a hug.

Here are a few other tips and suggestions:

You may feel nervous or awkward prior to and during the first few meetings. Not to worry! In any situation involving other people, it takes a little while to feel a sense of belonging.

Remember that nothing is written in stone. You and the other members of the group may find even better ways for creating the environment you want. Be flexible.

If the group size is over four, you may want to make a rotating 'leader of the week' who helps move the evening along.

Support each other by sharing from a place of power rather than from a victim mentality. No 'Woe is me' responses are to be encouraged. The objective is to help each other find solutions, to help each other take responsibility and to change what doesn't seem to be working. Group discussion is great, but judgement is to be avoided. Of course, *under no circumstances is physical violence ever to be tolerated*.

Those who get the most out of a group are those who commit to being there regularly, being there on time and being there when someone needs them. Don't be upset if members drop out. This is a frequent occurrence in group situations. Decide at that time if you want to enlist more members or continue as a smaller gathering.

Please note: Self-help groups are not therapy. If a member appears to be embroiled in a problem that is overwhelming, it is important that the group encourages him or her to seek therapy.

Here is a true or false checklist for each member of the group to answer on a regular basis. If any of the responses are 'false', they need to be discussed. This makes sure the integrity of the group is being maintained.

THE GROUP   true or false

1 ... helps me feel stronger.   ....

2 ... helps me feel more loving to
      myself and others.   ....

3 ... does not allow the victim mentality.   ....

4 ... encourages Higher-Self solutions.   ....

5 ... encourages me to take responsibility
for my actions and reactions. ....

6 ... does not allow whining. ....

7 ... uses all emotions as tools for
self-discovery. ....

8 ... does not tolerate hurtful acts
of any kind. ....

9 ... does not allow blame, only solutions. ....

10 ... discourages 'You poor thing'
responses. ....

11 ... gives feedback gently and supportively
rather than angrily or judgementally. ....

12 ... In most sessions, I feel I learn
something helpful. ....

13 ... I see that my feelings are nothing
to be ashamed of.

14 ... People in the group seem to really
care about each other's growth. ....

15 ... No one is ever made to feel foolish. ....

16 ... The group helps me *lighten up*. ....

17 ... I trust the others in the group. ....

18 ... I feel the group is a safe place to
help me move from Lower-Self to
Higher-Self thinking. ....

I have enjoyed the group process in many stages of my life
and I encourage you to try it too.

What the group gives me is safety and constructive feedback. We have formed an alliance here that feels very comfortable and very strong. I used to be really unsure of myself with other men but, slowly, as I learn to feel more powerful, I'm learning to communicate 'out there' as well.

**From a men's group
in Dare to Connect**

For the first time, there is equality. In the past, I was either being helped or helping. There was always a weaker and a stronger person. I find now my friendships are based on mutuality. Sometimes one person is weak and sometimes one is strong, and we help each other.

**From a women's group
in Dare to Connect**

PART IV
The Toolbox for Fear-Less Living

I am now tuning in to the best of who I am: my Higher Self. I open my heart and allow powerful and loving energy to flow through me. I am aware that my life makes a difference and that every action I take can help to heal the hurts within and around me.

1

REPLACE THE CHATTERBOX

My favourite spiritual tool is the affirmation. An affirmation is a strong, positive statement telling us that *'All is well'* – despite what the Chatterbox, the voice of the Lower Self, may be telling us. It is a very powerful tool to help us push through even the worst of our fears.

I have used affirmations so often and for such a long time (over twenty-three years) that I often find them roaming inside my mind throughout the day, keeping me in a positive, loving state. And if I find myself feeling fearful or upset about any situation in my life, I begin repeating an appropriate affirmation over and over again until peace envelops me like a warm blanket.

For example, one of my favourite affirmations is, *'It's all happening perfectly.'* When I repeat this affirmation over and over again, I can feel the fear and upset disappearing and I let go of my need to control everything around me. (I joke that I am a recovering 'control freak'.) For me, 'It's all happening perfectly' is a shortened version of:

> 'My mind cannot see the larger picture, the Grand Design. I will simply trust that all things happen for a reason and I will learn and grow from whatever life brings me. Therefore, even if a certain situation is not going the way I want it to go, *it is all happening perfectly.'*

Keeping the meaning of the affirmation 'It's all happening perfectly' in mind, let's play with it for a little while. First, think about something that you are fearful about. Write it down.

I am fearful about

....

....

....

....

....

....

Now that you have identified a particular fear, take a deep breath and say, out loud or silently, IT'S ALL HAPPENING PERFECTLY ten times (with your eyes open or closed, whichever is more comfortable for you):

IT'S ALL HAPPENING PERFECTLY.
IT'S ALL HAPPENING PERFECTLY.
IT'S ALL HAPPENING PERFECTLY.
IT'S ALL HAPPENING PERFECTLY.
IT'S ALL HAPPENING PERFECTLY.
IT'S ALL HAPPENING PERFECTLY.
IT'S ALL HAPPENING PERFECTLY.
IT'S ALL HAPPENING PERFECTLY.
IT'S ALL HAPPENING PERFECTLY.
IT'S ALL HAPPENING PERFECTLY.

If you are anything like me, the repetition of this sentence creates a wonderful sense of peace. If this was not your experience, not to worry! Perhaps this affirmation is not for you. Also, you might be asking, 'How can it be happening perfectly when it isn't going the way I want it to go!?!' As you continue with the exercises in this book, the answer will become clearer.

As you practise affirmations over a period of time, you will find they are a powerful way of silencing the Chatterbox. Understand that this voice of doom and gloom, the Chatterbox, will probably never go away completely; it is a companion that will be with you for a long, long time. Therefore, I suggest you give it a name. Choose a name that will make you laugh every time you think about it. Remember, we have to lighten up!

My Chatterbox is named ....

Now that you have named your Chatterbox, your goal is to observe when it is there, laugh and say 'Hello', and then tune into a Higher way of thinking. Repeating your favourite affirmations helps you tune into that Higher way of thinking.

The beauty of affirmations is that they can be done anywhere, anytime, without any extra materials and in the privacy of your own head – even though you may be surrounded by people. They can also be written, spoken and/or typed into your computer (if you have one). While a computer is considered by some to be a spiritually empty machine, I consider it to be very spiritually rich indeed.

With the computer, as opposed to a pen and paper, I can close my eyes and experience a meditative state while touch-typing my affirmations, thus strengthening their power in my mind. I can then print them out and put them in a very visible place. With my computer I can also be creative about the size of affirmations, the colour and the style.

It's amazing how confident I can become as the affirmations of my Higher Self flow through my fingertips. I often do this process before I start my writing and it is wonderfully effective in getting my Chatterbox out of the way so that I can write from my Higher Self, the best of who I am.

You can read many books about affirmations and notice that different authors give conflicting advice. So let me add to the pot of opinions about how affirmations should be used, with the understanding that in the end, it is up to you to choose the kinds of affirmations that feel right for you.

Most of the time, affirmations are more powerful when stated in the present tense, for example, 'I AM CREATING A WONDERFUL LIFE' instead of 'I *will* create a wonderful life'. The former says we are *already* making it happen. And, indeed, by using affirmations or any of the exercises in this book, you are *already* in the process of improving the quality of your life.

However, as with all exceptions to the rule, there are occasionally times when the future tense works as well. Another of my favourite affirmations is 'I'LL HANDLE IT', which, of course, is in the future tense. This affirmation can give you an enormous sense of peace when the frightening 'What ifs' come up in your life. For example:

What if I get ill? *I'll handle it!*
What if I don't get the job? *I'll handle it!*
What if something happens to my child? *I'll handle it!*

Really get a feeling of the power of these three little words, 'I'll handle it!' Whether you believe it or not, you really *can* handle whatever life brings you in the most creative and ful-filling ways . . . once you get the hang of listening to the voice of the Higher Self.

Right now think of five 'What ifs' that take away your peace and, after each one, write in big and bold letters *I'll handle it!* as I have done in the above example:

1. What if:

....

....

(Don't forget to write 'I'll handle it!' after your 'What if'!)

Yes! You will handle it!

2. What if:

....

....

Yes! You will handle it!

3. What if:

....

....

Yes! You will handle it!

4. What if:

....

....

Yes! You will handle it!

5. What if:

....

....

Yes! You will handle it!

This wonderful affirmation, 'I'll handle it!', always cuts off my Chatterbox in mid sentence when my 'What ifs' come up – and makes me aware that I, indeed, do have a huge amount of power inside me (as we all do!) to handle *whatever* comes up in my life. As I explained earlier, *if you knew you could handle anything that life were to hand you, what would you have to fear? Nothing!*

Don't be concerned if you don't believe the affirmations you are saying. Maybe you don't feel 'I can handle it!' but it has been demonstrated that just saying, thinking or writing positive thoughts makes us stronger in every way, *whether we believe the words or not.*[1]

Also, I have found that if you say affirmations often enough, you will ultimately believe them. Affirmations are a form of 'acting-as-if'. If you act-as-if long enough, your mind lets in the *possibility* that something is so. And ultimately, it *is* so.

A bonus: As you begin to repeat affirmations over and over again, your interaction with the outside world subtly changes. For example, when you say, 'I am powerful and I am loving and I have nothing to fear' often enough, you act differently, stand differently and react to the outside world differently. And you are treated differently. You draw healthier energy into your being. Affirmations are very powerful indeed.

Affirmations are best stated as a positive rather than a negative, such as, 'I am now building my confidence' rather than, 'I am no longer putting myself down'. Again, you can sometimes find exceptions that make you feel good. For example, I often say to myself, 'Not to worry!' which comes from the following saying I learned in England a long time ago:

> Not to worry . . .
> Not to fret . . .
> All is well . . .
> But not just yet!

I love to say this to myself when I am running out of patience. It makes me laugh and it builds my sense of trust about the future. And so does the shortened version, 'NOT TO WORRY!'

Some prefer affirmations that are long; some prefer them short. While I use both, I prefer short ones. When they get too convoluted they are not as easy to use and sometimes hard to remember. As I have already explained, short affirmations are really a condensation of a longer thought. As long as you keep the larger meaning in your mind, the shorter version is very effective.

I personally don't like affirmations that are too specific, such as, 'By December, I am creating a job in advertising that will pay me at least $70,000.' There is nothing wrong with setting such goals but, as I will discuss in a later chapter, letting go of outcomes is an important element of pushing through fear. Using such a specific affirmation always leaves us open for disappointment. You may get that job . . . or you may not! (Exercise 4 (see p. 81) gives you a Higher-Self 'qualifier' that you can use when creating specific goals to protect you from disappointment.)

Creating such specific affirmations also implies no trust in the Grand Design. You've heard the saying, 'Life is what happens when you've made other plans.' That's the Grand Design in action. If you don't get the job, it is for a reason. Perhaps there is something better out there for you at this particular time in your life. A more appropriate affirmation might be, 'I trust I will find a job that is for my Highest good.' It may be that job in advertising; it may not.

Affirmations help put things in perspective and build your sense of trust in yourself and the Grand Design. Again, it is important to experiment until you find the affirmations that work best for you. When something inside you says, 'Yes, that affirmation makes me feel good!', that's one to put on your practice list.

There are many categories of affirmation to help us push through fear. The following describes some of these and gives you an opportunity to create some of your own:

AFFIRMATIONS OF PURPOSE
We become powerful in the face of our fears when we have a sense we make a difference in this world. Affirmations of

purpose communicate the truth that we are all meaningful participants in this universe and that we are worthy of giving and receiving love. Some affirmations of purpose are:

I KNOW THAT I COUNT AND I ACT AS THOUGH I DO.
I SPREAD WARMTH AND LOVE EVERYWHERE I GO.
I AM A HEALING FORCE IN THE UNIVERSE.

Right now, create three affirmations of purpose that have meaning for you:

1. ....
2. ....
3. ....

AFFIRMATIONS OF SELF-RESPECT

We become powerful in the face of our fears when we are aware of the strength and beauty we hold inside. Most of us never feel good enough. No wonder we are fearful! Affirmations of self-respect sound like this:

I STAND TALL AND TAKE RESPONSIBILITY FOR MY LIFE.
I AM GOOD ENOUGH.
I CAN HANDLE ALL THAT HAPPENS IN MY LIFE IN A
    LOVING AND POWERFUL WAY.

Create three affirmations of self-respect that have meaning for you:

1. ....
2. ....
3. ....

AFFIRMATIONS OF SERENITY AND TRUST

We become powerful in the face of our fears when we know we can handle whatever life brings us and that we can trust the Grand Design. Affirmations of serenity and trust sound like this:

> I LET GO AND I TRUST.
> I RELAX KNOWING I CAN HANDLE ALL THAT NEEDS
>   TO BE HANDLED.
> I PEACEFULLY ALLOW MY LIFE TO UNFOLD.

Create three affirmations of serenity and trust that have meaning for you:

1. ....
2. ....
3. ....

AFFIRMATIONS OF GRATITUDE AND ABUNDANCE

We become powerful in the face of our fears when we focus on the abundance in our lives. Most of us have a 'scarcity mentality' which causes us to fear we will never have enough. Affirmations of gratitude and abundance show us how much we already have, despite the outer circumstances of our lives.

> I AM THANKFUL TO THE MANY PEOPLE WHO CON-
>   TRIBUTE TO MY LIFE.
> I FOCUS ON MY MANY BLESSINGS.
> I AM FINDING THE GIFT IN ALL EXPERIENCES.

Create three affirmations of abundance that have meaning for you:

1.
2.
3.

AFFIRMATIONS OF POWER AND LOVE
We become powerful in the face of our fears when we are aware of the immense amount of power and love we hold inside. How about:

> I AM POWERFUL AND I AM LOVING.
> I AM POWERFUL AND I AM LOVED.
> I AM POWERFUL AND I LOVE IT!

Three more affirmations of power and love are:

1.
2.
3.

Hopefully, you are now getting a feel for the art of creating affirmations. You will also find that I have provided you with daily affirmations in your '30-Day Power Planner' (Part VI)[2].

Now, how do you incorporate these wonderful affirmations into your daily life? Here are a few suggestions. You may want to choose some affirmations that have particular meaning to the events of the day. For example, if you are going to an important business meeting, a few good affirmations are:

> I KNOW THAT I COUNT AND I ACT AS IF I DO.
> I TRUST I WILL SAY EXACTLY WHAT NEEDS TO BE SAID.

I AM POWERFUL AND I AM LOVING AND I HAVE
NOTHING TO FEAR.

If you are spending the day with your mate, affirmations of
appreciation are relevant:

I AM AWARE OF MY MANY BLESSINGS.
I AM CREATING A WONDERFUL DAY.
I AM GRATEFUL FOR THE LOVE I GIVE AND RECEIVE.

Affirmations can be said while you dress, shower, exercise,
while you are sitting at your desk or taking care of your
children and, of course, as you are going off to sleep. Find
the times that work best for you and form the habit of saying
your affirmations at these times.

One of my students created a rolodex of various affirmations which she kept in her car. As she was driving (and making sure she did so safely!), she said each affirmation ten
times, and flipped the page to the next . . . and the next . . .
and the next. By the end of her trip, she felt very powerful
indeed!

In the beginning, it is best to use affirmations intensively
until they become part of your everyday thinking. This is easy
since affirmations take no time out of your day. They simply
replace one kind of thinking for another, the voice of the
Chatterbox with the voice of the Higher Self. A very good
exchange!

There is only one difficulty with the beginning stages of
using affirmations (and all spiritual exercises): we forget to
use them! Does that sound familiar? To help you remember,
I suggest you:

Create index cards with your favourite affirmations and
put them anywhere they will capture your attention – on
your desk, in your car, on your mirror and so on.

After practising affirmations for a while, you will find them automatically kicking in when you are feeling stressed about situations in your life. This is good news. It means that all your practice is starting to pay off. You are slowly acquiring the habit of Higher-Self thinking. When you get to the point where you *always* remember to pull an affirmation into your thinking when facing difficulty, you have come a long way in reducing your fear.

You are beginning to see that you are more than the voice of gloom and doom. You are also the voice of power, confidence, love and all good things. And when you develop the habit of listening to the best of who you are, your ability to push through fear increases enormously. So begin using this wonderful tool, the affirmation, this very minute. Why don't you begin with:

> I AM CREATING A WONDERFUL LIFE.
> I AM CREATING A WONDERFUL LIFE.
> I AM CREATING A WONDERFUL LIFE.
> I AM CREATING A WONDERFUL LIFE.
> I AM CREATING A WONDERFUL LIFE.
> I AM CREATING A WONDERFUL LIFE.
> I AM CREATING A WONDERFUL LIFE.
> I AM CREATING A WONDERFUL LIFE.
> I AM CREATING A WONDERFUL LIFE.
> I AM CREATING A WONDERFUL LIFE.

I am forty-three years old. Only a month ago, my wife died and I lost my job. At this time of double tragedy, your book helped me grow more in a month than I ever have in my whole life. While there are difficult moments, you have made me realize that 'I can handle it' and at the very least become a strong and more effective person.

B. D.
Witchita, USA

At the age of thirty-seven, I was lost and didn't know who I was and what I wanted. When I read your book, I was determined to start acting on your suggestions and not just put the book aside. One of my favourite affirmations is also one of yours, 'It's all happening perfectly!'

On the way to a second interview for a job I really wanted, I turned my radio off and started talking to myself, telling myself all sorts of good things about my 'self', getting myself really up for this interview. It worked. I was psyched by the time I got there. I got the job! I have been saying affirmations more and more every day, because they really do work! There are times when I still hear my 'Chatterbox' saying 'old' things, but the new positive messages are increasing daily. It is all happening perfectly!

S. T.
Sheffield, UK

2

ASK YOUR HIGHER SELF

If you let it, your Higher Self will always tell you the truth, which is: 'You are powerful and loving and you have nothing to fear.' Your Lower Self, on the other hand, will always tell you the big lie: 'You are *not* powerful and loving and you have much to fear!' So let's continue looking at ways to empower the voice of the Higher Self and diminish the voice of the Lower Self.

Let me introduce you to this exercise by giving you two questions to ask yourself – and then give you practice in answering them:

What would my Lower Self say about this?
and
What would my Higher Self say about this?

Here is an example: You've just interviewed for a job you want very badly. Let's listen to what the voice of the Lower Self might be telling you:

'I shouldn't have talked so much about my kids. Maybe they'll think I'm not qualified for the job. I really want this position. I bet I won't get it. Then what will I do? I was so nervous. I really didn't do my best. I hope I looked OK. My skirt was a bit short. Oh, why didn't I wear my trouser suit? It's much more businesslike. Maybe I'm too old to go back to work. I'm sure they want someone younger.' (And on and on and on.)

Now let's listen to what the voice of the Higher Self might be telling you:

> 'This job is not my life. I did my best. If I get the job it's wonderful. If I don't get the job, that's wonderful, too. It would mean this job is not for me and there is something else out there waiting for me. I am finding exactly what I need. I trust the Grand Design. I let go and trust that everything is happening for my Highest good!'

Now I ask you, which voice would make you feel and behave more powerfully in the face of your fears? Which voice would bring you a sense of confidence and peace? Which voice would you rather listen to?

If you said the voice of the Lower Self, we would have to conclude that you love pain and there would be no need for you to go any further in this book! Yet I am 99½% certain you would rather listen to the voice of the Higher Self! So why don't you? As I've already explained, your HABIT is to listen to the Chatterbox, the voice of your Lower Self! And now you are working to break this self-destructive habit.

So let me give you some practice in seeing the contrast between Lower-Self and Higher-Self thinking. Practice will make you more aware – awaken you to the reality that you are being run by your Chatterbox. With this awareness, you can quickly change the channel and tune instead into the voice of your Higher Self where you will find courage and peace of mind.

Right now think of something that could go wrong in any area of your life and simply 'role play' the voice of doom and gloom and the voice of power and love. If you don't have enough room for your answers in the space allotted, use a special notebook that you can refer to often.

Example:
I am worried about:

_____*Ageing*_____

What would the voice of my Lower Self say about it?

> '*I am getting older now. Ageing is horrible. I wish my body were young again. Look at these wrinkles. Who could love a face that's old? I hate it. Pretty soon no one will want to be around me. When I was young, I could dance all night. Now I don't have the energy. Why do people have to age? I wish I could be young forever.*'

What would the voice of my Higher Self say about it?

> '*I love ageing. My children are grown and I'm now free to do the things I've always put off doing. I'm glad I joined a gym. I don't think I've ever been in such great shape. I'm going to learn all I can about keeping myself in the best of health. I have so much to look forward to. I learn and grow every day of my life. I wouldn't want to go back one day. Why would I want to go back?*'

I know people who think about ageing from the point of view of the Lower Self and those who think about ageing from the point of view of their Higher Self. Can you guess which are having the more joyful, exciting and wonderful lives? Need I say more?

Now think of some of your own worries and role play the possible responses of your Lower Self and Higher Self. Exaggerate and have a lot of fun with this.

I am worried about:

_____

What would the voice of my Lower Self say about it?

....

....

....

....

....

What would the voice of my Higher Self say about it?

....

....

....

....

....

I am worried about:

_____

What would the voice of my Lower Self say about it?

....

....

....

....

....

What would the voice of my Higher Self say about it?

....

....

....

....

....

I am worried about:

_____

What would the voice of my Lower Self say about it?

....

....

....

....

....

What would the voice of my Higher Self say about it?

....

....

....

....

....

I am worried about:

_____

What would the voice of my Lower Self say about it?

....

....

....

....

....

What would the voice of my Higher Self say about it?

....

....

....

....

....

Don't you love the *choice* you can have in thinking about various situations in your life? Obviously, choosing to listen to the voice of the Higher Self guarantees you a life filled with power, joy and love.

Because Lower-Self thinking is a difficult habit to break, it helps to have reminders wherever they can be seen. For example, I keep a card on my desk that says, 'Susan, what would your Higher Self say about this?' (Yes, my desk is covered with all sorts of reminders!) And when I find myself upset about something, this card reminds me to 'wake up' and listen to the best of who I am, not the worst. And, often, I take the time to type into my computer my Higher-Self response to a situation, just as you have done in the above exercise, and immediately feel a sense of peace.

I would suggest that right now you create a few signs on index cards, just as you did with your affirmations, and put them in areas you can see them – on your mirror, in your car, on your desk, in your diary and anywhere else you will see them that say:

WHAT WOULD MY HIGHER SELF SAY ABOUT THIS?

Then, if you find yourself upset about something in your life, this reminder will wake you up to the fact that you are simply listening to the voice of the Lower Self. Start with little things. For example, when your Chatterbox won't stop complaining about the lousy traffic, the card on your dashboard will remind you to ask what your Higher Self would say about this situation. You would get an answer such as the following:

> Great! I have more time to listen to this beautiful music. I can relax and think about the blessings in my life. Moving at such a snail's pace, I can watch the beautiful sunset. I can actually have a great time enjoying the beauty of the moment.

Any moment of the day, in any situation in your life, you can now choose to listen to the healthier, stronger and joyful part of who you are. *The voice of your Higher Self . . . how sweet it is!*

*Thank you for putting me back in touch with a self
I used to know but had lost contact with somewhere
down the line, a self that enjoys: lives, loves, loves
living and believes that life is a tree whose branches
go on and on expanding. You reminded me of the
spiritual part I had once known but which had become
crowded out by a negative Chatterbox so loud nothing
else could be heard. And with the warning: 'Unless you
regain contact with that spiritual part, you will remain
in permanent discontent', an awareness of my
responsibility dawned. It was my choice: my life was
already abundant; I could choose to notice the
rewarding and fulfilling things which came my way
each day or I could live in torment with my negative
Chatterbox. I chose to say Yes! to the universe. The
difference in my life is amazing!*

*C. T.
Sydney, Australia*

3

SAY 'YES!' TO LIFE!

This exercise comprises one magical word. And that word is 'YES!' Right now, nod your head up and down and softly say YES! to yourself over and over again until you feel like screaming it joyfully to the world.

YES! is more than a word, *it is an attitude of spiritual fullness*, the essence of Higher-Self thinking. The word YES! as I am using it says that, 'No matter what happens in my life, I'll make something wonderful out of it.' I know this sounds difficult when one thinks about the possible losses and disappointments life often brings but saying YES! is the antidote to the fear that more often than not accompanies these losses and disappointments.

I talk about my experience of breast cancer in all my work, hoping it will bring comfort, not only to others in the same situation but also to those who live in fear of this very prevalent disease. Because I am so open about it, I received an award from the Associates of Breast Cancer Studies, a wonderful organization that raises money for the John Wayne Cancer Institute in Santa Monica, California.

I'd like to share with you part of my acceptance speech. It demonstrates how the attitude of YES! can exist even with something as potentially devastating as breast cancer. It demonstrates that the beauty is always there *if you look for it*. That's the key. If you don't look for it, you remain stuck in a victim mentality: the helpless, hopeless feeling that results from Lower-Self thinking. And you miss out on so many of the opportunities that even a disease such as cancer can bring.

Also in this acceptance speech, you will notice the

humour. We take things much too seriously in our present day world. Laughter can bring a lot of joy where sadness once prevailed:

'. . . Tonight I am being honoured with the Spirit of Discovery award. This such an apropos award for me because, impossible as it may seem, breast cancer has indeed offered me a great opportunity for discovery. In fact, I can go so far as to say that breast cancer has been one of the most enriching experiences of my life. Now don't look at me like I'm crazy. Let me explain.

For many years before my illness, I was teaching my students how to say YES! to life . . . how to say YES! to whatever life hands them and to find the beauty no matter how difficult a situation may be. I had learned this philosophy of life after reading and re-reading *Man's Search for Meaning* by Viktor Frankl which, as many of you know, describes his experience in a concentration camp. He had seen and experienced the worst life had to offer, and yet he learned that one thing no one could ever take away from him was his *reaction* to whatever life handed him. And his choice was to react to his horrible experiences in a way that brought much enrichment to his life and to the world.

After the first reading of this inspiring book, I said to myself, 'If he can say YES! to something as horrible as a concentration camp, which included the worst kind of treatment one can imagine and the loss of his loved ones, then I can say YES! to anything.' And I've tried to live my life with a great big YES! in my heart ever since.

So there I was lying in my hospital bed thirteen years ago and saying to myself, 'OK, Susan, you have a choice now. Are you going to see yourself as a victim, or are you going to say YES! and find the blessing in something as frightening as breast cancer?' With my YES! philosophy, I thankfully chose the latter. Trust me when I tell you I didn't understand immediately what possible blessings there could be in breast cancer, but when I set my sights on looking for the blessings instead of the negatives, I found so many . . . and I am still counting. Let me share some of these blessings with you:

1. I was dating my present husband, Mark, at the time. I wasn't quite sure where I wanted this relationship to go. I was the 'no-need' woman, incredibly independent. He was the workaholic, work coming before everything. When I was diagnosed with breast cancer, he was able to see my vulnerability and dropped everything to be with me. I was able to see this incredible nurturer that emerged from deep within his soul . . . and I let myself take in all the gifts of love and caring he was giving. This experience was so meaningful to both of us that we decided we wanted to spend the rest of our lives together. So Mark and I married . . . and twelve years later it remains a marriage made in Heaven.

2. What else did I learn? This is for you women out there. I learned that sexuality had nothing to do with a breast. I have never had a breast reconstruction after my mastectomy simply because I did not want to incur any more trauma to my body. And when I look in the mirror, I do not feel mutilated as some magazine articles suggest I should be feeling. Rather I look at that scar and breathe a sigh of relief and gratitude knowing I've conquered a disease. I celebrate the fact that I am now healthy. And I feel just as sexual as I did before the mastectomy. I learned that sexuality is an attitude, a way of being. It has nothing to do with a breast. In fact, Mark says I look like a sexy pirate!

3. Another blessing. When Mark used to travel a lot on business, as a joke, I would often put one of my spare prostheses in his suitcase with a love note. He often

bragged that he was the only man he knew who could take his wife's breast with him whenever he goes away!

4. At the time, I also asked myself if there were any negative emotions I was holding within that could cause disease in my body. As I looked, I couldn't help but notice I was still holding on to a lot of old anger, like many women still hold today. While I liked being angry (it was a very pseudo-powerful feeling!) I decided it was time to let it go . . . to deal with the fear and pain that were lurking behind the anger. I learned that anger can be a cop-out for not taking responsibility for my actions and reactions in life. I stopped casting blame; I took charge of my life; I honoured who I was and I learned how to open my heart. Wow! What a difference an open heart makes in your life! It lets in the sunshine instead of the gloom. My letting go of my anger was also the impetus to writing my second book, entitled *Opening Our Hearts to Men*.

5. Then there was the time I went for a mammogram. As I was paying my bill, the cashier said that it was 120 dollars. She looked again and said, 'Wait. It's only one side. That's 60 dollars.' And I shouted, 'YES! I even get to save some money!'

6. And then there's my teaching. Often when I talk about saying YES! to life, a student will say, 'That's easy with the little things. But what about the big things, such as cancer?' It's here that I can say, 'You sure can say YES! to cancer. I did!' And I tell my story.

7. And then there's the issue of ageing. Someone asked me recently if ageing bothered me. I said, 'Are you kidding! Once you've had cancer you celebrate every birthday with much greater joy than you ever did before. And so do the many people who love you.'

8. In many ways, cancer is like a wake-up call. It says one never knows how much time one has left in life. So

we should stop focusing so much on the future and pay more attention to the simple pleasures of everyday life. And that's what I have learned to do. That first cup of coffee in the morning. YES! The hot shower on the back. YES! The purr of the engine when the key is turned in my car. YES! The beautiful sun warming the very depths of my being. Heaven! I discovered that it's not the grand splashes of brilliance that define a beautiful life. It's the simple pleasures of the NOW. A wonderful lesson indeed. And it was this discovery that eventually led to my book *End the Struggle and Dance with Life*. You see, it's all grist for the mill!

9. And then there was the day I received a phone call from the ABCS asking if I would accept the Spirit of Discovery award. Would I accept it? YES!!! . . .'

I hope this little acceptance speech conveys in a meaningful way the enormous power in *looking for the good* in any situation in which we find ourselves, even one as potentially devastating as breast cancer. If we focus only on the negative, that's what we will get: the negative. If we focus on the positive, that's what we will get: the positive.

On a more dramatic note, I watch the profound contribution Christopher Reeve, who played the role of Superman, is making to this world. As you recall, a riding accident left him a quadriplegic. I remember the day I heard about his accident. I wondered whether he was going to dissolve into the misery of the situation or whether he was going to say YES! and emerge triumphant. Here was a powerful figure, a sex symbol, an athlete, faced with something as devastating as almost total paralysis and all the accompanying problems that go with it.

It didn't take long to realize that Christopher Reeve knows how to say YES! to life. He has made incredible discoveries about the real meaning of life and love. He has emerged as a symbol to all people that life can be beautiful, perhaps at times even more beautiful, in the face of great challenges. I'm sure, given the choice, Christopher Reeve would have chosen an easier pathway to growth. Who wouldn't? But he took the hand that life, the Grand Design, dealt him and created a magical scenario that brings hope to the hearts of many who watch in wonder.

I know it's very easy to say YES! when things go right for us. We get that job we wanted . . . YES! We find that relationship we wanted . . . YES! Our children are healthy and happy . . . YES! But the trick is saying YES! when things *don't* happen the way we want them to happen . . . when things are going badly. We can only do that when we realize there are blessings inherent in all things and our task is to find them.

Before you start practising the wonderful art of saying YES! to life, please let me clear up a misunderstanding some have about seeing life in a positive, life-affirming way. *Saying YES! to life is not about denial of fear and pain*. I'm sure Christopher Reeve has and continues to shed tears about losing such an important part of his being. I'm also sure Viktor Frankl shed tears while watching and experiencing the horrors of a concentration camp. I, too, shed tears when I found out I had cancer since it is, of course, a very frightening disease. But when they are the tears of YES!, tears are not bad. In fact, they are essential. (Only the tears of the 'victim' the tears of NO! are self-destructive.) In fact, denial of pain is dangerous to Body, Mind and Soul. It is *false* positive thinking. Real positive thinking is saying YES! to the fear and pain – realizing we will always get to the other side. We will learn and grow from it *all*.[3]

Now that you understand the concept of saying YES!, it's time for some practice. Right now, write down ten things that you are fearful of having happen in your life. After you write each fear-producing situation in the allotted space, say out loud (or to yourself) with strong conviction:

'I can say YES! to this. I refuse to be a victim. If this ever happens, I will find many blessings that will enrich my life.'

Really embrace the meaning of this powerful phrase as you are saying it!

1. I am fearful of:

....

....

....

(Repeat) 'I can say YES! to this. I refuse to be a victim. If this ever happens, I will find many blessings that will enrich my life.'

2. I am fearful of:

....

....

....

(Repeat) 'I can say YES! to this. I refuse to be a victim. If this ever happens, I will find many blessings that will enrich my life.'

3. I am fearful of:

....

....

....

(Repeat) 'I can say YES! to this. I refuse to be a victim. If this ever happens, I will find many blessings that will enrich my life.'

4. I am fearful of:

....

....

....

(Repeat) 'I can say YES! to this. I refuse to be a victim. If this ever happens, I will find many blessings that will enrich my life.'

5. I am fearful of:

....

....

....

(Repeat) 'I can say YES! to this. I refuse to be a victim. If this ever happens, I will find many blessings that will enrich my life.'

6. I am fearful of:

....

....

....

(Repeat) 'I can say YES! to this. I refuse to be a victim. If this ever happens, I will find many blessings that will enrich my life.'

7. I am fearful of:

....

....

....

(Repeat) 'I can say YES! to this. I refuse to be a victim. If this ever happens, I will find many blessings that will enrich my life.'

8. I am fearful of:

....

....

....

(Repeat) 'I can say YES! to this. I refuse to be a victim. If this ever happens, I will find many blessings that will enrich my life.'

9. I am fearful of:

....

....

....

(Repeat) 'I can say YES! to this. I refuse to be a victim. If this ever happens, I will find many blessings that will enrich my life.'

10. I am fearful of:

....

....

....

(Repeat) 'I can say YES! to this. I refuse to be a victim. If this ever happens, I will find many blessings that will enrich my life.'

Do you see that when you can say YES! to anything that happens or that you can imagine happening in your life, the fear is diminished? This doesn't mean the fear will go away, but it means you will find yourself incredibly powerful in the face of your fear.

So many people who lose their jobs, who lose someone they love, who become ill, who face death, and on and on and on, experience fear. But with an attitude of YES!, the fear is made powerless. It no longer has the ability to take away our deep sense of joy, meaning, appreciation, participation, power and love. YES! is a powerful word indeed!

Saying YES! saved my life. When my husband died four years ago, I thought I couldn't go on. But, thankfully, the urge to live is stronger than the urge to give up. As you suggested, I began looking for the blessings, even though I couldn't imagine any blessings could be found. He was my life.

Well, I found many blessings surround me when I keep my eyes open. Most of all, I found inner strength I never thought I had. Even being alone has its advantages. I'm doing things I never did as a married person, such as travelling to exotic places. Yes, life is good. Thank you for showing me how to live.

A. B.
Glasgow, UK

4

LET GO OF OUTCOMES

Perhaps one of the most damaging misinterpretations of present-day spiritual teachings is the idea that if you create a clear, detailed picture of your dream – whether it be in the area of career, relationship, health or whatever – and you visualize it clearly, strongly and often enough, it will happen. Well, I'm here to tell you *it may happen . . . or it may not!* As the saying goes, 'Life is what happens when you've made other plans!'

Over the years, I've learned that there is nothing wrong with visualizing something clearly, strongly and often enough . . . BUT . . . it is essential to add one vital Higher-Self element to our visualization that makes the difference between intense disappointment and peaceful discovery. This Higher-Self element is to:

LET GO OF THE OUTCOME!

We have to cut the cord. We have to let go of our expectations. We have to 'un-set our heart'. A heart that is set on something is rigid, doesn't know how to flow and often gets broken. When we un-set our heart, we are free. When we let go of the outcome, we are free to rise, to 'float' peacefully and gracefully to the Highest part of who we are. If whatever we have so carefully visualized happens, so be it. If it doesn't happen, so be it. This is freedom in its highest sense! It is this mind-set that allows us to let go of fear and bring peace into our hearts.

Ultimately, we learn that 'life', or the Grand Design, has a much broader view as to what is best for our Highest good.

It serves our peace of mind to trust but trust is difficult. Instead, when the Grand Design takes over and doesn't accommodate our wishes, we are disappointed and upset – and sometimes very fearful. We lament our bad fortune and see ourselves as the VICTIM, the most helpless place to be. When we learn how to let go of outcomes and trust the Grand Design, peace is restored. Again, it's all about accessing the Higher Self, which is what this book is all about.

To teach you how to let go of outcomes, I've created an exercise that I find very useful and easy to do. Let me first demonstrate before you try it. Suppose the following was your specific expectation for the future:

'By the time I am thirty-five years old, I will be happily married and have two children, one boy and one girl. The person I marry will be loving and gentle, and we will have enough money to enjoy the best life has to offer.'

This is a nice goal but the crazy-making problem is, it may happen or it may not. What is needed to restore peace of mind is the addition of the Higher-Self 'qualifier' to help you let go of the specific outcome. Again, let me demonstrate:

'By the time I am thirty-five years old, I will be happily married and have two children, one boy and one girl. The person I marry will be loving and gentle, and we will have enough money to enjoy the best life has to offer . . . OR WHATEVER ELSE THE GRAND DESIGN HAS IN STORE FOR ME. IT'S ALL HAPPENING PERFECTLY FOR MY HIGHEST GOOD.'

The words I've added are very spiritually powerful. They bring in the element of *TRUST*. So many times, we don't quite understand why certain things happen in our life, but if we simply learn to *turn it over*, we relax into the peace of our

Higher Self, knowing it is all happening for our Highest good.

This Higher Self qualifier placed at the end of any of your stated goals for the future cuts the cord that creates the emotional pain that comes from rigid expectations. It also helps you trust the future. It may not turn out the way you want it to turn out . . . and that's OK. You are open to all possibilities.

We can look at our expectations about how our children will grow up; about getting a promotion; about our car starting; about how dinner will turn out; about everything in our lives. As long as we add our Higher-Self qualifier: '. . . or whatever the Grand Design has in store for me. It's all happening perfectly for my Highest good', we are letting go of the outcome and, as a result, we won't be disappointed.

Now it's your turn to create ten specific goals or expectations of your own, big or small, and write them in the following spaces provided. I've already added the Higher-Self qualifier that allows you to let go of the outcome of any of your hopes and dreams.

1.

Or whatever the grand design has in store for me. it's all happening perfectly for my Highest good.

2.

Or whatever the grand design has in store for me. it's all happening perfectly for my Highest good.

3.

....

....

Or whatever the grand design has in store for me. it's all happening perfectly for my Highest good.

4. ....

....

....

Or whatever the grand design has in store for me. it's all happening perfectly for my Highest good.

5. ....

....

....

Or whatever the grand design has in store for me. it's all happening perfectly for my Highest good.

6. ....

....

....

Or whatever the grand design has in store for me. it's all happening perfectly for my Highest good.

7. ....

....

....

Or whatever the grand design has in store for me. it's all happening perfectly for my Highest good.

8. ....

Or whatever the grand design has in store for me. it's all happening perfectly for my Highest good.

9.

Or whatever the grand design has in store for me. it's all happening perfectly for my Highest good.

10.

Or whatever the grand design has in store for me. it's all happening perfectly for my Highest good.

Now re-read out loud what you have written, adding the Higher-Self qualifier that will allow you to let go of all your expectations in a trusting and powerful way.

It is a good idea to memorize the qualifier. Then every time you find yourself creating an expectation for the future, you know how to let go and trust by adding those wonderful words: '. . . or whatever the Grand Design has in store for me. It's all happening perfectly for my Highest good.'

Who understands the mystery of it all? Certainly not me. But I do know that when I trust the Grand Design, I can let go. I can rest easier. I can search for the opportunity in all situations in my life. I can live into the triumph of all situations of my life. And so can you. Trust that it is all happening perfectly – and you will find that it is!

I had been hesitating about my long-term relationship for the previous two years and suddenly found the strength to finish it in great harmony, felt strong enough to buy an apartment on my own and refurbish every bit of it alone (and on a budget) while working full time. I push my limits every day further and still find it hard to believe that, against the handyman's limiting advice, I found the 'guts' to do the plastering, paint my very high ceilings despite the vertigo I usually have, carry out my creative ideas with confidence, etc. I feel I am coming out of a time when I was sort of depressed because of external pressures, discovering with enthusiasm how good it feels to free oneself.

As you promise in Feel the Fear and Do It Anyway, *feelings of true love and trust do come when we reach this new way of life. I now think, 'OK. I'm dead scared, but it is not life threatening so I'm going to try it. Fear of failure seems more frightening than failure itself. I risk nothing by trying.' That is my new motto and I love myself every day a bit better for discovering so many things in my exploration of new fields. This leads me to encourage my friends to do the same and increases my real deep love for them.*

Well, thank you so much for communicating your ideas and enthusiasm to others.

S. A.
San Diego, USA

5

PRACTISE MAKING NO-LOSE DECISONS

For many of us, having to make decisions creates a huge amount of fear! The 'What ifs' run rampant in our Lower-Self minds, creating all sorts of insecurities. What if it doesn't turn out the way I want it to?' 'What if I should have chosen the other pathway?' A classic No-Win situation!

I can assure you that if you were to change channels and listen to the voice of your Higher Self, you would be able to create a No-Lose scenario instead. The following steps take you a long way in reaching that goal:

I) *Repeat Over and Over again the No-Lose Philosophy of the Higher Self.* And that philosophy is:

'*I can't lose* – regardless of the outcome of the decision I make. I look forward to the opportunities for learning and growing that *either choice* gives me. Any road I take is strewn with riches for my highest good.'

When we realize we will learn and grow no matter how things turn out, the pressure in decision-making is greatly reduced. You can see why I call this the No-Lose approach to decision-making: this No-Lose way of thinking guarantees that all our decisions will be *right* decisions.

To imprint the No-Lose philosophy in your mind, list ten decisions you want to make. These decisions can be about small or large matters: the principle is exactly the same. Again, I've added an important Higher-Self message that will free you from worrying about all the possible outcomes.

TEN DECISIONS I WANT TO MAKE

1. ....

....

(Repeat) 'I can't lose – regardless of the outcome of the decision I make. I look forward to the opportunities for learning and growing that *either choice* gives me.'

2. ....

....

(Repeat) 'I can't lose – regardless of the outcome of the decision I make. I look forward to the opportunities for learning and growing that *either choice* gives me.'

3. ....

....

(Repeat) 'I can't lose – regardless of the outcome of the decision I make. I look forward to the opportunities for learning and growing that *either choice* gives me.'

4. ....

....

(Repeat) 'I can't lose – regardless of the outcome of the decision I make. I look forward to the opportunities for learning and growing that *either choice* gives me.'

5. ....

....

(Repeat) 'I can't lose – regardless of the outcome of the decision I make. I look forward to the opportunities for learning and growing that *either choice* gives me.'

6. ....

....

(Repeat) 'I can't lose – regardless of the outcome of the decision I make. I look forward to the opportunities for learning and growing that *either choice* gives me.'

7.

(Repeat) 'I can't lose – regardless of the outcome of the decision I make. I look forward to the opportunities for learning and growing that *either choice* gives me.'

8.

(Repeat) 'I can't lose – regardless of the outcome of the decision I make. I look forward to the opportunities for learning and growing that *either choice* gives me.'

9.

(Repeat) 'I can't lose – regardless of the outcome of the decision I make. I look forward to the opportunities for learning and growing that *either choice* gives me.'

10.

(Repeat) 'I can't lose – regardless of the outcome of the decision I make. I look forward to the opportunities for learning and growing that *either choice* gives me.'

II) *Do your Homework*. A No-Lose attitude puts us on the right path. In addition, there are helpful steps to take before and after making a decision. Let me demonstrate. First, choose one of the bigger decisions you have to make.

Should I .... ?

OR

Should I .... ?

Before you make a final decision, it is important to learn as much as you can about your options. The following are a few questions to ask yourself. Be creative and adapt these questions to your particular situation:

Who can I talk to about this decision to be made?

Friends/Family ....

....

....

Professionals ....

....

....

Others who have had experience in the field ....

....

....

Where can I find reading material to give me more information?
(Remember libraries and the Internet)

....

....

What else can I do to learn as much as I can about either choice?

....

....

....

....

....

III) *Do Some Soul Searching.* After you've gathered as much information as you can, then it is time to ask yourself the following questions which allow you to look inward. These are essential for finding harmony in your life:

What are my priorities in life with regard to beliefs, values, money, comfort and the like? Which priorities would make me happier, give me greater satisfaction and harmony with the truth of who I am? Which would make me feel good about who I am as a human being? Spent a lot of time thinking about this:

My priorities in life are:

....

....

....

....

....

....

....

....

Now look at the decision to be made and ask yourself:
Which choice fits best with my priorities in life?

....

....

....

IV) *Trust your Intuition*. After you've done all of the above,
it is important to get a sense of which pathway *feels* right to
you on an intuitive level. I believe that deep within us lies a
spiritual intelligence, an incredible inner wisdom that can
guide us to where we need to go in all areas of our lives – and
that is our intuition. The logical mind is very valuable and we
need it in our day-to-day dealings in the world but if we listen
only to the logical mind, we are selling ourselves short.

To me, intuition is one of our most valuable resources.
Too many amazing things have happened in my life when
I listened to my intuition for me to disregard its wisdom. It's
as though this part of me is connected to the Grand Design
and, when I listen, I know exactly what to do and where to
go for my Highest good.[5]

Even if, after you've done all your homework, and your
logical mind tells you to go one way, your intuition (your
'gut') may be telling you to go the other. In my experience,
your intuition is usually a beacon to remarkable and unfore-
seen opportunities in your life. In fact, when you learn how
to listen more intently to your intuition, 'miracles' will seem
to happen in your life, as they have happened in mine! So
ask yourself:

What does my 'gut' (my intuition) tell me to do? What *feels*
right?

....

....

....

....

Now that you've I) learned the No-Lose philosophy, II) done your homework, III) looked at your priorities in life, and IV) listened to your intuition, it is now time to make your decision. (Not to worry! This is only practice. But do try it!)

Knowing that either decision is the *right* decision, my choice is to:

....

Congratulations! You did it! Now it's time for a very important step. You'll recognize it from the last section.

V) *Let Go of the Outcome!* Yes, it's time to cut the cord – to un-set your heart as to how the choice you made will turn out. You say to yourself:

'Even if it doesn't turn out the way I want it to, I will look for all the blessings to be found. I will learn and I will grow. It is all happening perfectly for my Highest good.'

Even if the stock market goes down when you've just invested, or the job doesn't turn out well, or the movie you chose was lousy, or whatever . . . you will make your decision work for you by finding value in it all. Now, to make the process complete:

VI) *Lighten Up!* You can't take it all too seriously! In the Grand Scheme of things, in the realm of the Higher Self, nothing is really that important. As the saying goes: 'DON'T

SWEAT THE SMALL STUFF . . . AND IT'S ALL SMALL STUFF'. Our Lower Self, of course, makes a big deal about it! In the realm of the Higher Self, it's just all part of the process of learning how to let go and trust the Grand Design.

Remember those three powerful words: 'I'LL HANDLE IT!' Say to yourself over and over again: *Whatever happens as a result of my decision . . .*

I'LL HANDLE IT!
I'LL HANDLE IT!
I'LL HANDLE IT!
I'LL HANDLE IT!
I'LL HANDLE IT!
I'LL HANDLE IT!
I'LL HANDLE IT!
I'LL HANDLE IT!
I'LL HANDLE IT!
I'LL HANDLE IT!

Yes, you certainly will handle it. In addition, you will learn from it, you will grow from it, you will become stronger as a result of it. No matter how it all turns out, you will use the outcome to create marvellous new insights into living a glorious life.

It is truly worth the effort involved in learning how to make No-Lose decisions. As I point out in *Feel the Fear and Do It Anyway*, the alternative – the No-Win approach – is certainly less desirable as you can see from the following:

THE NO-WIN MODEL
Before a decision is made:

1. Focus on the philosophy of the No-Win model which is: 'If I make the wrong decision, it will ruin my life!'
2. Keep listening to your mind drive you crazy.

3. Paralyse yourself with anxiety as you try to predict the future.

4. Don't trust your impulses – listen to what everyone else thinks.

5. Feel yourself drowning in the dread of having to make a decision.

After a decision is made:

6. Create anxiety by trying to control the outcome.

7. Convince yourself you made the *wrong* decision.

8. If it does work out, keep wondering if it would have been even better the other way.

Need I say more?! Why be miserable when you can be happy? It is so healing to live with the mind-sets that whatever happens as a result of your decision, even if it doesn't fit your picture of what it's 'supposed to be', you made the *right* decision!

> *Sometimes you are in the right place at the right time. This was it for me. The cover of your book,* Feel the Fear and Do It Anyway, *caught my attention; something inside said buy it! I did and I'll probably never be the same again. THANKS!*
>
> *T. R.*
> *Seattle, USA*

6

EXPAND THE COMFORT ZONE

I often suggest a wonderful action exercise that will help you build your confidence and, of course, ultimately reduce your fear. I call this 'Expand the Comfort Zone'.' You will find it fun as well as effective . . . and a little scary! YES!

Let me refresh your mind about the Comfort Zone. If you think about it, each of us lives in our own cocoon. This cocoon is what I call the Comfort Zone. When we take a risk and go beyond what is comfortable, discomfort, often in the form of fear, takes over. For example, you may be comfortable eating alone in fast-food restaurants but uncomfortable eating alone in more formal ones. You may be comfortable talking to your boss about holidays but uncomfortable asking him or her for a rise. In terms of becoming the best you can be and moving forward with your life, it is important that you keep expanding your Comfort Zone to encompass more of the richness that life has to offer.

Everyone's Comfort Zone is different, depending on the circumstances of their lives. For example, a woman who is used to taking care of herself financially frequently has a far greater Comfort Zone about money than a woman who is dependent on her husband for all of her income. A person who has grown up in the countryside usually has a far greater Comfort Zone in the woods than a person who has grown up in the city.

When I divorced my first husband there were many zones of comfort I had to push through: my first date, my first dinner party without a mate, my first trip alone and so on. Each time I took a little step into the unknown, I felt stronger and stronger. And my Comfort Zone kept getting larger and larger and larger.[7] In fact, I can't believe how large it's become! Over the years, I have learned that one never runs out of Comfort Zones to push through. Life is always handing us new opportunities through which to expand and grow, and some of them are very scary indeed!

For those who have read *Feel the Fear and Do It Anyway*, you may remember the following chart which clearly demonstrates what happens as we take more and more risks:

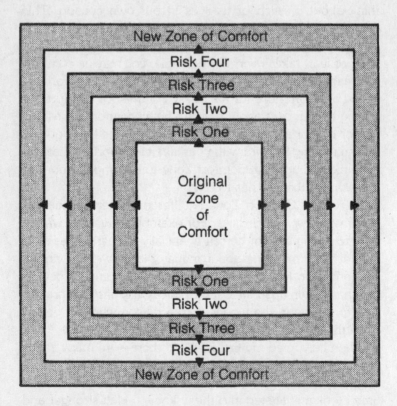

You'll notice that with each risk taken, the box which represents the boundaries of your life gets larger and larger. With each expansion of your Comfort Zone, your confidence grows and grows. The more confidence you have, the more you are able to push yourself from pain to power – and the more you are able to push yourself through the fear that is stopping you from moving forward with your life.

One way to expand your Comfort Zone in an easy manner is to take a little risk each day. By building your confidence gradually, you will ultimately be ready for that BIG risk you want to take – or are forced to take because of unexpected happenings in your life.

TAKING A RISK A DAY IS THE SAFETY NET YOU CREATE FOR YOURSELF THAT REASSURES YOU OVER AND OVER AGAIN THAT YOU CAN HANDLE WHATEVER HAPPENS IN YOUR LIFE.

Before you begin working on your plan to take a risk a day, I want to emphasize an essential paragraph also contained in *Feel the Fear and Do It Anyway*:

'The risks I am talking about do not include physically dangerous acts, such as speeding in a car or taking recreational drugs. Nor do they include risks that infringe on the rights of other people, such as making a pass at someone's mate or, for that matter, robbing a bank. Not only could you end up unpopular, dead or in prison, but you would also be moving yourself far to the left side of the Pain-to-Power chart. These kinds of acts are not empowering because they do not have any integrity or love – for one's self or others – behind them. Without these ingredients, it is impossible to build your sense of self-worth. Hence your ability to handle fear would be greatly diminished.'

Now that I have said that, let's put some of this risk-taking into practice.

1. *First think of thirty risks you would like to take in the coming month, one per day, and list them on the next page.* Remember, they don't have to be major risks, until you are ready. Begin with the small ones and watch your confidence grow.

If you can't think of all thirty right now, which may be the case, just think of a few to get you started. Then, as you go through each day, *notice what you are avoiding* because of your fear and add it to the list. Eventually you will come up with thirty risks to be taken.

You can include risks from all areas of your life: career (making a cold sales call), relationship (calling someone for a date) or living in general (taking an evening class). These may even seem like big risks to you now. Not to worry! Start as small as you wish. As you continue to take one a day, soon they will all seem much more manageable!

2. *Each evening, pick one of the risks that you intend to take the following day.* You can take them in any order you wish and, of course, if you are feeling particularly brave, you may want to take more than one on any given day – or you may find yourself taking one that isn't even on the list. If you do, you can count it as the risk of the day and add it to your list of thirty.

3. *Schedule your risk of the day in your diary as you would a doctor's appointment (which may be one of your risks!)* Or put one per day in the allotted spaces of your '30-Day Power Planner' (see page 159).

30 RISKS TO EXPAND MY COMFORT ZONE

1.
2.
3.
4.
5.
6.
7.
8.
9.
10.
11.
12.
13.
14.
15.
16.
17.
18.
19.
20.
21.
22.
23.
24.
25.
26.
27.
28.
29.
30.

4. *After you complete one of the risks, check it off on the allotted space of the check list (see opposite page) and say to yourself, 'Yes! I did it! What's my next risk?'* You will find that each one makes you willing to expand further and that the taking of risks gets easier and easier as time goes by. Remember, *action builds your confidence.*

Important tip: If you find yourself hesitating a great deal in taking a risk on a given day, repeat the following affirmation over and over again.

WHATEVER HAPPENS, I'LL HANDLE IT!

If he or she rejects you for that date, you'll handle it. If you don't get that raise, you'll handle it. And so on. Now try to take that risk again. If you are still unable to do so, just put it aside. This is not a risk-taking contest! Don't beat yourself up. As you continue working the exercises in this book, one day you'll take all the risks you will ever want to take.

CHECK LIST OF RISKS TAKEN

1. .... Yes! I did it! What is my next risk?
2. .... Yes! I did it! What is my next risk?
3. .... Yes! I did it! What is my next risk?
4. .... Yes! I did it! What is my next risk?
5. .... Yes! I did it! What is my next risk?
6. .... Yes! I did it! What is my next risk?
7. .... Yes! I did it! What is my next risk?
8. .... Yes! I did it! What is my next risk?
9. .... Yes! I did it! What is my next risk?
10. .... Yes! I did it! What is my next risk?
11. .... Yes! I did it! What is my next risk?
12. .... Yes! I did it! What is my next risk?
13. .... Yes! I did it! What is my next risk?
14. .... Yes! I did it! What is my next risk?
15. .... Yes! I did it! What is my next risk?
16. .... Yes! I did it! What is my next risk?
17. .... Yes! I did it! What is my next risk?
18. .... Yes! I did it! What is my next risk?
19. .... Yes! I did it! What is my next risk?
20. .... Yes! I did it! What is my next risk?
21. .... Yes! I did it! What is my next risk?
22. .... Yes! I did it! What is my next risk?
23. .... Yes! I did it! What is my next risk?
24. .... Yes! I did it! What is my next risk?
25. .... Yes! I did it! What is my next risk?
26. .... Yes! I did it! What is my next risk?
27. .... Yes! I did it! What is my next risk?
28. .... Yes! I did it! What is my next risk?
29. .... Yes! I did it! What is my next risk?
30. .... Yes! I did it! What is my next risk?

Without going into too much boring detail, I was suffering from anxiety attacks. I want to tell you about the words that helped me most. First, your suggestion to push through and enlarge that area of comfort around you. I tried with small things to begin with as you suggested (like going over a bridge) and feeling that great feeling after facing the fear. I was able to build my confidence and ability to know, whatever it is, I'll handle it! And then, I was able to face increasingly scarier fears. (Of course, I was sweating and my heart raced, but it was worth it!) I'm working with other fears as well and I know you really must push through each one to get to the other side and feel that wonderful feeling.

When I face these fears now, big or small, I am reminded of myself as a daring fifteen-year-old: the old me, the one who used to do things before having too many preconceived fears. I am not 100% there yet, but I'm in the 90% area and have to thank you!!!

S. B.
San Francisco, USA

7

UNCOVER THE PAYOFFS

It is hard to understand why people choose to remain in situations that cause them unhappiness. On a surface level, it doesn't make any sense but when we dig a little deeper we find good reasons why negative situations are worth keeping. I call these reasons the 'payoffs'.

My experience is that once you can discover the underlying payoffs for being in a certain situation, it's much easier to move past them. *Awareness often creates action*. Let me give you a few examples of what payoffs look like.

Suppose you hate your job. What could the payoffs be for staying? Surely your Lower Self can find many 'victim' excuses why you must stay in a job you hate, such as the lousy job market, or nobody else would hire you because of your colour or gender. Poor you! Victim! Nothing you can do about it. Victim! But, looking beyond the blame and beneath the surface, is it possible that, as miserable as it is, you are comfortable in the job? Or you like the salary? Or you like the location? Or, most importantly, you don't have to test yourself in a new environment with new responsibilities?

And what about the payoffs for staying in a bad relationship? Again, your Lower Self can find many 'victim' excuses why you must stay in a relationship you hate, such as that a breakup would hurt the children, or your mate needs you too much. Is it possible that, as miserable as the relationship is, you're afraid to be alone? Or you're afraid to make it on your own financially? Or you're afraid you'll never find someone else?

The underlying payoff of all 'victim' excuses, of course, is that by staying 'stuck', we don't have to push through the fear and take responsibility for our lives. We don't have to pull ourselves out of the muck and mire. We can just sit there and play the role of the victim.

You might be asking, 'Why don't I just stay in a state of blame? It sure is easier that way.' My answer is that there are many good reasons for giving up the payoffs and honouring who you are as a human being. A few of those reasons are:

HAPPINESS,
PEACE OF MIND,
SATISFACTION,
JOY,
SELF-RESPECT,
CONFIDENCE,
A LIFE WELL-LIVED.

Need I say more?! So, right now, name one area of your life you would like to change but in which you feel stuck. It could be something to do with career, relationship, children, parents, lifestyle or whatever is appropriate in your life.

That area is ....

Now ask yourself, 'What payoff or payoffs would I have to give up to change my situation?' That is, 'What "comfort" do I need to give up?' Or, 'What fear do I have to push through to change this situation in my life?' (This is not a numerical contest. Sometimes one payoff is enough to keep us stuck indefinitely!)

....

....

....

....

Tip: If you can't find payoffs, ask a friend to help. Sometimes they are obvious to others but masked from our own vision. You might be surprised to discover your friends know more about your motives than you do!

Now ask yourself, 'What would I gain by letting go of the payoffs and taking the responsibility of pulling myself out of this situation, which doesn't work for me?'

....

....

....

....

Given the pluses and minuses, ask yourself: 'Is it worth giving up the payoffs and taking responsibility for pulling myself out of the muck and mire?' (Yes or no) ....

If your answer is 'NO!', not to worry. Perhaps it's not yet time to make the changes you want to change.

If your answer is 'YES!', your next step is to ask yourself what steps you have to take to change that situation in your life. You will recognize this as a form of expanding your Comfort Zone, but targeting it on one specific area of your life. Remember to keep the steps very, very small.

Then, list these steps on the chart on the following page. Understand that you can add to the list anytime you realize a further step must be taken. Note that the space to the left of the numbers is for you to make a check mark once that action is taken.

When you have made the list as complete as you can, begin taking action, checking off items on the list and watching your power grow. One day, you will be ready to make the big change with a confident and happy heart. Repeat this exercise in all areas of your life where you feel stuck.

I AM NOW WILLING TO TAKE RESPONSIBILITY FOR MY LIFE. I WON'T BE FOOLED ANY LONGER BY THE PAYOFFS THAT HAVE KEPT ME STUCK. WHAT STEPS DO I HAVE TO TAKE TO CHANGE THIS SITUATION THAT IS NOT WORKING IN MY LIFE?

.... 1. ....
.... 2. ....
.... 3. ....
.... 4. ....
.... 5. ....
.... 6. ....
.... 7. ....
.... 8. ....
.... 9. ....
.... 10. ....
.... 11. ....
.... 12. ....
.... 13. ....
.... 14. ....
.... 15. ....
.... 16. ....
.... 17. ....
.... 18. ....
.... 19. ....
.... 20. ....

An Important Note: Some situations in your life may seem overwhelmingly difficult to change. In this day and age, it is acceptable to seek professional help which can give you important insights and help you take the necessary steps. You are not a 'crazy' person if you go for help. You are very wise indeed! Over the years, I know that I have moved past many obstacles in my life because I sought the help of professionals. And if I ever feel really stuck again, I wouldn't hesitate to seek professional help once more.

If it is your choice to get some help, my suggestion is to find a health professional who understands the concepts of Higher-Self thinking . . . of taking responsibility for your own life. Any professional who promotes the Lower-Self qualities of guilt, blame, anger and so on, is not the person for you. Just keep looking. You will definitely find someone to help.

Aid is also available in books, tapes, workshops, seminars and so many other avenues. We live in a time of spiritual richness when it comes to learning about inner growth. Take advantage of it all. At one time in my life, I was a 'workshop addict', and it surely paid off in terms of a healthier, happier, more productive, joyful and loving life.

Be patient with yourself. Sometimes it takes time, even a number of years, to make desired changes in our lives. Don't discount the concept of readiness. I always liken readiness to the rhythms of nature. When it's time for flowers to bloom, they bloom. And, as long as you are learning the secrets of Higher-Self living, desired changes in your life will ultimately happen. Remember, IT'S ALL HAPPENING PERFECTLY!

I am a part-time freelance writer and, about the same period I purchased your book, I was working on a story about battered women. So much of your information spoke directly to their situation that I recommended it to the local shelter as a resource manual. At that point I was in the process of starting my own freelance writing business, which I hoped would allow me to quit my full-time position and find more time for my clients and my own writing. Every time I worried about leaving the security of a steady paycheque, I would haul out your book and re-read Chapters 4 and 7. Then I would go back to cold-calling and marketing, and working on what small projects were dribbling my way.

Well, it's been about six months now and, although I'm not quite ready to quit my job, I have enough clients to make it more a reality than a pipe dream. My birthday is soon, and I hope my present to myself will be full-time self-employment!

B.C.
Charlotte, USA

8

TAKE BACK YOUR LIFE!

As you might already have surmised, I feel very strongly about the concept of taking responsibility for our lives! I am concerned that the victim mentality seems to be spreading like an epidemic. We seem to be competing to see who can be the most pathetic! My suggestion to combat this problem is that we constantly remember what Victor Frankl so movingly taught us in his incredible book, *Man's Search for Meaning*. This, as I mentioned earlier, describes life in a concentration camp. Listen to his words of great wisdom:

> 'Everything can be taken away from a man but one thing: the last of the human freedoms – to choose one's attitude in any given set of circumstances, to choose one's way. The way in which a man can accept his fate and all the suffering it entails, the way in which he takes up his cross, gives him ample opportunity – even in the most difficult circumstances – to add a deeper meaning to his life.'[8]

Yes, we have a choice! We can choose how we want to react to any situation. The victim attitude has no place in a healthy life because it is a diseased and powerless one. Therefore let's get to work on choosing our attitude, thereby taking responsibility for our experiences of life.

What does taking responsibility for our experiences of life really look like? It means not blaming anyone for anything you are doing, being, having or feeling. 'NOT BLAMING ANYONE, SUSAN? BUT IT REALLY IS HIS (HER OR ITS)

FAULT!' *No one!* Not your parents, not your children, not your mate, not the economy, not the government and so on. You are responsible for your *reaction*, despite what is happening around you.

All the exercises in this book are about you taking responsibility for your experience of life and creating something meaningful out of whatever life has handed you in the past or will hand you in the future. That's what Higher Self thinking allows us to do. This exercise and the next focus directly on this important aspect of our lives.

Let me begin with a very common activity of everyone's Lower Self: complaining! Complaining is a big clue that you are not taking responsibility for your life. Complaining will not change things in your life; only action will. And if there are certain things you cannot change – the weather, the service in the restaurant, the behaviour of others and so on – complaining will only make it all worse. How do we stop this very prevalent habit of complaining?

First, ask yourself: 'What big things and little things do I complain about? Then list them in the following space. Really spend time thinking about this and LIGHTEN UP!

....

....

....

....

....

....

....

....

To enlarge that list, begin carrying a pen and a little note-book. Each time you find yourself complaining – to yourself or to a friend – about anything, write it down. The only problem with this exercise is that COMPLAINING FOR MANY OF US IS SUCH AN EMBEDDED HABIT THAT WE DON'T EVEN NOTICE WHEN WE ARE COMPLAINING! Trust me on that one!

To help you become aware, I suggest you enlist the help of one of your friends. Agree that for one entire week there will be no complaints. Instead, focus on the good things that are occurring in your lives. I always joke that, in the beginning, you will have very silent conversations! You will also laugh a lot as you realize how often you are griping about one thing or another.

It is important that your friend point out to you when you are complaining, and vice versa. You might be wondering, if you are not complaining, what you should talk about instead? My answer is that you focus on the great things happening in your life: all the blessings that surround you. (More about that on pages 135–143.) Keep practising with your friend until your conversations become upbeat and filled with appreciation.

Now it's time to ask yourself a few very important questions. Dig deep for the answers and if you need extra space, write in a notebook.

Who are the people or situations I blame or have blamed for upsets in my life?

....

....

....

....

One by one, what do I blame them for now or have blamed them for in the past? (Remember to use a notebook if you need extra space.)

....

....

....

....

....

....

....

....

....

When I blame them, how do I feel?

....

....

....

....

Do the majority of my responses to the last question resemble those on the Lower-Self side of 'The Choice is Mine' chart at the end of this chapter? YES OR NO   ....

What words can my Higher Self say to me that will help me take responsibility for my reactions to what has happened to me? (Refer to Exercise 2 (p. 49) if you need a refresher.)

....

....

....

....

....

....

....

When I take responsibility, how do I feel?

....

....

....

....

Do the majority of my responses to the last question resemble those on the Higher-Self side of 'The Choice is Mine' chart at the end of this chapter? YES OR NO   ....

I believe the choice is yours. You can listen to the Lower Self and have a life filled with blame and scarcity – or you can listen to the Higher Self and have a life filled with power and love. Yes, the choice is definitely yours.

THE CHOICE IS MINE

When I am tuned into my Higher Self:	*When I am tuned into my Chatterbox:*
I trust	I try to control
I appreciate	I don't notice my blessings
I love	I need
I care	I am insensitive
I am at peace	I am in a turmoil
I am creative	I am blocked
I count	I don't know I count
I attract	I repel
I make a difference	I don't make a difference
I give and receive	I take
I am involved	I am bored
I am filled up	I am empty
I am confident	I am filled with self-doubt
I am content	I am dissatisfied
I see big	I have tunnel vision
I live now	I wait and wait
I am helpful	I am helpless
I am joyful	I never enjoy
I go with what is	I am always disappointed
I forgive	I hold resentment
I am relaxed	I am tense
I am alive	I am a robot
I love getting older	I am being passed by
I am powerful	I am weak
I am protected	I am vulnerable
I am on the path	I am off-course
I let go	I hang on
I have so much	I am poor
I am connected	I am lonely
I am excited	I am afraid

*I was really down in a deep hole, being run by my
Chatterbox. One night I said to myself, 'I will either
have to kill myself or just do what it takes to live.' The
next day I read your book, letting it make a difference.
Whenever I feel myself slipping away from my Higher
Self, I read the page called 'The choice is mine' and
I am able to reconnect with my higher part. Thank you
so much for helping me life.*

*T. L.
Melbourne, Australia*

9

FIND 'FRIENDLY' FRIENDS

Thankfully, none of us have to stand alone in this big wide world. Your friends can be an important part of your support system and it is one area of most people's lives that needs cultivation. But what kind of friends do I mean?

I'm not talking about the kind of friends that pull you down. I'm not talking about the kind of friends that try to keep you from moving forward. I am talking about the kind of friends that say, 'Sure, you can do it.' 'Go for it.' 'Even if it doesn't work out, there is always something out there for you.' 'Whatever happens, you'll learn a lot.' And so on. I like to think of those who hold you back as Lower-Self friends and those who support your growth as Higher-Self friends. And it's important to pay attention to the difference.

You may be surprised to find that the people you've considered your friends may not always be capable of having your best interests at heart. Let's look at this.

List six friends you often talk to about the happenings in your life. If you can't list six, that's nothing to be upset about. Some of us have just one or two intimate friends.

....

....

....

Now, ask yourself, which of these friends are 'Be careful' friends (Lower-Self ones) and which are 'Go for it' friends

(Higher-Self ones)? Which hold you back and which encourage you to go forward?

Right now, list which are your 'Go for it' friends and which are your 'Be careful' friends.

                Go for It!   Be Careful!

....

....

....

Now you know who to talk to when you want to move forward in your life! It's not that those who are the more 'Be careful' oriented can't be friends. Simply don't go to them when you need courage.

What if all your friends belong in the 'Be careful' category? That's simple: *Make new friends who belong in the 'Go for it' category*, but before you set out on this exciting adventure, a little self-inventory is necessary. Friends are a great mirror of our own behaviour. Always remember the Universal Law: LIKE ATTRACTS LIKE.

So, right now, answer the following questions as truthfully as you can:

1. *Generally speaking, are you a 'Go for it' friend or a 'Be careful' friend?* That is, do you encourage your friends to go for what they want or do you constantly warn them of possible failure in whatever they are attempting to do? Check which best describes your interaction with friends.

I am a 'Be careful' (Lower-Self) friend.   ....
                            OR
I am a 'Go for it' (Higher-Self) friend.   ....

2. *Do you spend a lot of time complaining to your friends?* Are your conversations of the 'moan and groan' variety or are they of the 'positive and appreciative' variety?

I spend a lot of time complaining to my friends.
(Lower Self)
                                                              ....

OR

Our conversations are usually upbeat even when one of us is going through a bad time. We laugh through our tears. (Higher Self)
                                                              ....

If you gave the Lower-Self answer to both, not to worry! No judgement here! Your goal now is to learn how to pull yourself up into the Higher-Self category so that you have a greater chance of drawing Higher-Self friends into your life. How do you do this?

Begin by thinking of ten Higher-Self qualities you would like to have in your friends and write them down here. Some possible Higher-Self qualities are: positive, helpful, caring, appreciative, enthusiastic. These are in contrast to Lower-Self qualities such as: negative, self-involved, insensitive, stuck. You get the picture.

Ten Higher-Self qualities I would like to have in my friends are:

1. ....

2. ....

3. ....

4. ....

5. ....

6. ....

7. ....

8. ....

9. ....

10. ....

You may be surprised by what I want you to do with these then Higher-Self qualities. Are you ready? What I want you to do is to *pick up the mirror and begin developing these Higher-Self qualities in yourself*. As you 'become' what you would like to find in your friends, it will be easier and easier to draw into your life the kind of friends you want. As I've already told you, LIKE ATTRACTS LIKE! So become the observer of your behaviour and start creating a Higher-Self way of being in the world. The exercises in this book will surely help.

Also, *become the observer of all your conversations with friends*. When you notice yourself thinking in a Lower-Self way, just say to yourself, 'Ah, I'm thinking Lower-Self thoughts . . .' Again, there's no judgement here (or anywhere for that matter). You will soon become aware of your Lower-Self patterns and you can begin changing them into Higher-Self patterns.

This doesn't mean upsetting things in your life don't have to be changed. They do. But it is much more productive and loving to confront the things that need to be changed from a Higher-Self perspective instead of a Lower-Self one. The greatest benefit that can be derived from our friendships occurs when we help each other to be the best that we can be, as opposed to buying into each other's complaints and feelings of helplessness. And you can take the lead.

Now that you are on the way to becoming a Higher-Self kind of friend, how do you go about meeting other Higher-Self friends? You can begin by listing six people you have admired as acquaintances and would like to get to know as friends. Hopefully these are people who are living their lives in a way you respect.

....

....

....

Now is the tough part for many of us. *Give them a call and invite them for lunch or dinner.* What do you say? Simply say, 'I admire you as a person and would love to get to know you better. Why don't we get together for lunch?' If you are anything like I was when I began developing a circle of strong friends, I was very nervous making those calls. I was such an insecure person that I didn't believe that these terrific people would want to have lunch or dinner with me. But I 'felt the fear and did it anyway' and created a lot of wonderful new friends.

It is important to risk rejection and take responsibility for making the first approach. If he or she doesn't seem interested after a few calls, move on to the next person. Always keep in mind that no matter how anyone acts towards you, you are a worthwhile person. Trust me when I tell you that, as you become more positive, you also become more magnetic and people will love to have a friendship with you.

Here is another way to meet new friends. List some of the things you love to do in life or have wanted to do, for example, riding, being involved in politics, going back to college, travelling, attending personal growth workshops, and so on:

....

....

....

Now search your newspapers for activities that revolve around those listed interests and sign up for one or more. Be willing to go to these activities alone. When we recruit friends to go with us, we tend to avoid reaching out to meet new people. Also remember if you are feeling uncomfortable, that's good! You're feeling the fear and doing it anyway!

Tip: If you have a hard time reaching out to other people, the group process (see pages 27–31) can help enormously. It teaches that we are not alone in our feelings and that it is beautiful to connect meaningfully with others. The group process certainly created much enrichment in my life.

Just keep in mind that when you have a circle of powerful and loving friends, you can breathe a sigh of relief. When in need, they will be there to support you – as you will be there to support them. What a great safety net for all situations that may occur in your life!⁹

10

CREATE A GRID OF LIFE

The Grid of Life has reduced the fears of many of my students. I am so happy to be able to give you some practice in making it work in your life. Before we start, let me give you an explanation of the Grid of Life (or a refresher course if you have read *Feel the Fear and Do It Anyway*).

Too many of us allow one area of our life to be emotionally all-consuming. For some, it's relationship; for others it's work; or perhaps it's children. When anything is emotionally all-consuming, we are setting ourselves up for a great deal of fear.

Look at the following diagram which is meant to represent someone's life-space, perhaps yours. It is a life-space that has made RELATIONSHIP supremely important.

LIFE SPACE 1

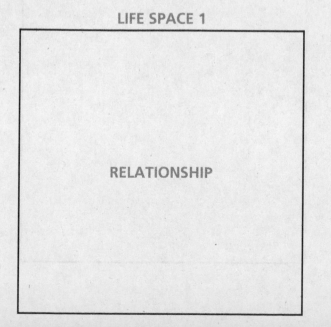

RELATIONSHIP

As long as the relationship is going beautifully, all *seems* well. But suppose the relationship ends, either because of divorce, death or a simple parting of the ways between two unmarried people. What does the life-space look like then? Life Space 2 demonstrates the grim reality. Yes, that's what it looks like. What does it feel like?

EMPTY! LONELY! FEARFUL!

And think about this: when a relationship is of such all-consuming importance, we don't have to wait for it to break up to experience fear! Fear is felt *every day* when we contemplate the *possibility* of the relationship ending. Because of this fear, we are often consumed by all kinds of relationship-destroying feelings, such as jealousy, resentment, anger and the like. With such feelings entering our interactions with

LIFE SPACE 2

our loved ones, we are creating what we are so fearful of happening. Do I detect another NO-WIN situation?

If work is emotionally all-consuming, what happens when you lose your job or retire? Your life becomes:

EMPTY! LONELY! FEARFUL!

Can this explain why so many men and more and more women die or commit suicide when they retire? 'Who am I? Why am I?' are the questions they ask themselves. And too many cannot find the answer.

Or if a child is emotionally all-consuming, what happens when he or she leaves home? Or if something tragically happens to the child? What does life become for the parent?

EMPTY! LONELY! FEARFUL!

Again, I have seen people fall apart, never to pull themselves back together again, when they experience the loss of a child.

If I've depressed you with all this negativity, let me assure you:

IT DOESN'T HAVE TO BE THIS WAY!

The diagram on the next page demonstrates a way of sculpting your life to minimize your fears and maximize your joys. I call it the '"Fear-Less" Grid of Life'. Notice I don't say 'Fearless'. As you have already learned, fear will always accompany us on our journey through life. But we can certainly create a way of being in this world where we can Fear less – where fear does not affect our ability to move forward in a healthy, life-affirming way.

'FEAR-LESS' GRID OF LIFE

1 PERSONAL GROWTH	2 RELATIONSHIP	3 CAREER
4 FAMILY	5 SPIRITUAL GROWTH	6 FRIENDS
7 CONTRIBUTION	8 ALONE TIME	9 PLAYTIME

Gorgeous! It certainly looks a lot more nourishing than the life-spaces I presented earlier. And notice what happens to this life-space when we take away Relationship (see opposite). Yes, there's a little hole in our heart that makes us feel the hurt once in a while. But does the loss of the relationship make us feel totally empty, lonely and fearful? Hardly! There's too much going on in the rest of our lives for that to happen.

Some of my students have lamented that they have all the elements in their lives that the Fear-Less Grid demonstrates but relationship (or work, or children) is still of all-consuming importance, dominating too much of their emotional life. What are they to do?

As I showed in *Feel the Fear and Do It Anyway*, two more ingredients are necessary to make the Grid of Life fill you up on an emotional level. The first is that you need to KNOW YOU COUNT in all areas of your life. You need to

'FEAR-LESS' GRID OF LIFE

1 PERSONAL GROWTH	**2**	**3** CAREER
4 FAMILY	**5** SPIRITUAL GROWTH	**6** FRIENDS
7 CONTRIBUTION	**8** ALONE TIME	**9** PLAYTIME

know your presence makes a difference to the world around you. It's amazing to me that so many people don't understand that their lives really do make a difference! Some say to me, 'But, Susan, I really don't feel that I count.' If you are someone who also feels that way, let me tell you what I have told so many others. '*Act-as-if you do make a difference!*' In every area of your life, ask yourself a very key question:

WHAT WOULD I BE DOING
IF I WERE REALLY IMPORTANT HERE?

When you ask yourself this question, you will come up with some pretty amazing answers. Eventually you 'live into' the realization that YOU REALLY ARE IMPORTANT IN THIS VERY NEEDY WORLD.

The second ingredient you need to have is 100% COMMITMENT to all areas of your life that are important to you.

For example, when you are with your family, make sure you are with them 100% – not reviewing work, reading the newspaper or wishing you were somewhere else. If you commit to giving 100% to all areas of your life, your senses of focus, excitement, participation, enjoyment, fulfilment and happiness come alive, perhaps for the first time. And what a glorious feeling that is!

I call KNOWING THAT YOU COUNT and 100% COMMITMENT the '*Magic Duo*'. And, indeed, they create magical results. Now that you understand the theory, it's time for you to create your own Fear-Less Grid of Life. What do you want it to include? You may include the ingredients in the one on page 116 or any other ingredients that are important to you.

I have one request. Please, please, please include the two categories of 'Contribution' and 'Spirituality' in your life space. These are very important areas. As far as contribution is concerned, I am convinced that when we commit to something larger than we are, we are on the pathway to self-respect, confidence, caring and love. So I encourage you to make Contribution an important part of your Grid of Life.

How do you begin? Ask yourself, 'What activity in the community could I care very deeply about?' It could be in the area of the environment, literacy, hunger, peace, a community project, politics or whatever. When we contribute to such endeavours we are reminded every day that we are important members of this global family. This is a tremendous impetus towards fear-less living.

And then, proceed to contribute in your own way, step by step. You will be amazed at how much distance your loving light can cover in this step-by-step manner. And how fearless you feel with each step you take.

Your Spirituality box is about your commitment to spiritual growth. It is about your daily exercises, such as those found in this book, for moving yourself from the Lower to the

Higher Self. I would put this box right in the centre of your grid, as your commitment to the Higher Self is one area that affects all the other areas of your life. These two boxes of your grid – 'Contribution' and 'Spirituality' – are very important parts of your life in terms of feeling wonderful about the person you are and the person you are becoming.

With the Magic Duo in mind, take the time right now to create your own Fear-Less Grid of Life below. As you begin, really think about how you would like to sculpt your life in a very meaningful and personal way.

After you've completed your grid, take some more time to ask yourself what you want each of your life choices to look like. For example:

....'S
(Your name)

'FEAR-LESS' GRID OF LIFE

1	2	3
4	5	6
7	8	9

Box 6 *Friends*

I want positive friends with whom I can share the good and the bad. We will give each other support when needed and applaud each other's successes.

Now it's your turn.

Box 1
I want this area of my life to look like this:

....

....

....

Box 2
I want this area of my life to look like this:

....

....

....

Box 3
I want this area of my life to look like this:

....

....

....

....

Box 4
I want this area of my life to look like this:

....

....

....

....

Box 5
I want this area of my life to look like this:

....

....

....

....

Box 6
I want this area of my life to look like this:

....

....

....

....

Box 7
I want this area of my life to look like this:

....

....

....

....

Box 8
I want this area of my life to look like this:

....

....

....

....

Box 9
I want this area of my life to look like this:

....

....

....

....

Now that you've given yourself an idea of what you want each area of your life to look like, begin taking action to create it that way. Remember *you are creating your life. You are not waiting for someone else to create it for you.* Also remember this: when you are taking action, your fear slowly diminishes.

With that in mind, let's take the example of FRIENDS. What *specific* action is needed to create a rich body of friends? Here are a few examples:

I am lessening the frequency of seeing any friends who pull me down.

I will call Alice, even though I am nervous of calling her. She always seems to be busy. I'll give it a try. If she says she is too busy, I will find others with whom I would like to share a friendship.

I will call at least one friend a day and let him or her know I am thinking about them.

I will be very present when I am with my friend Karen on Tuesday instead of wishing I was on a date with Bob.

And on and on and on. You get the picture.

Tip: Each time you mention an action, close your eyes and see yourself doing that particular action. As you create your Grid of Life, it is essential that you keep your 100% commitment in mind and that you remember that *you truly do count*. Also, as you plan your actions for a rich and rewarding life, ask yourself about each area of your grid. 'WHAT WOULD I BE DOING IF I REALLY COUNTED?' This important question will give you an amazing array of ideas you would not have thought of before!

So, right now, begin looking at each box in your Grid of Life and fill in, in the pages provided at the end of the chapter, the actions you need to take to make each area very meaningful and emotionally satisfying. Spend a lot of time thinking about this and add to the list when new ideas come into your mind. These new ideas are often wonderful messages sent to you by your Higher Self.

Obviously you can't take all these actions in one day! As you plan each forthcoming day, look at the actions you have committed to take and insert one or more from each category in your daily activities. Clearly, while work may occupy eight or more hours of your day, within those eight hours, how many of the other components can you include? Hourly affirmations; being kind and patient with co-workers; calling a friend during your lunch hour or other breaks to thank them or make plans. In the beginning, actually schedule time as you would a doctor's appointment for each component of your life. It's *that* critical to your health and happiness!

Don't put yourself down if you don't cover every item

every day of your life. There is room for much flexibility. If you have a deadline for work, or if a child is sick, or if you are on holiday, obviously other areas of your life will have to take a back seat for a while.

IT IS AN ATTITUDE OF FULLNESS AND ACTION THAT YOU NEED TO BRING INTO YOUR BEING.

Your Fear-Less grid is your entry into the attitude of fullness and action you are striving for. When you realize how rich your life truly is, there is little that can take away your sense of well-being. Always remember, LIFE IS HUGE! Enjoy it all!

BOX 1

> I commit 100% to this area of my life.
> I know that I count and I act as if I do.

If I really counted in this area of my life, what action would
I be taking?

....

....

....

....

....

....

....

....

....

....

....

....

....

....

....

....

BOX 2

> I commit 100% to this area of my life.
> I know that I count and I act as if I do.

If I really counted in this area of my life, what action would
I be taking?

....

....

....

....

....

....

....

....

....

....

....

....

....

....

....

....

....

....

BOX 3

I commit 100% to this area of my life.
I know that I count and I act as if I do.

If I really counted in this area of my life, what action would
I be taking?

....

....

....

....

....

....

....

....

....

....

....

....

....

....

....

....

....

....

BOX 4

> I commit 100% to this area of my life.
> I know that I count and I act as if I do.

If I really counted in this area of my life, what action would I be taking?

....

....

....

....

....

....

....

....

....

....

....

....

....

....

....

....

....

BOX 5

> I commit 100% to this area of my life.
> I know that I count and I act as if I do.

If I really counted in this area of my life, what action would I be taking?

....

....

....

....

....

....

....

....

....

....

....

....

....

....

....

....

BOX 6 ....

> I commit 100% to this area of my life.
> I know that I count and I act as if I do.

If I really counted in this area of my life, what action would
I be taking?

....

....

....

....

....

....

....

....

....

....

....

....

....

....

....

....

....

....

....

BOX 7

> I commit 100% to this area of my life.
> I know that I count and I act as if I do.

If I really counted in this area of my life, what action would I be taking?

....

....

....

....

....

....

....

....

....

....

....

....

....

....

....

....

....

BOX 8 ....

> I commit 100% to this area of my life.
> I know that I count and I act as if I do.

If I really counted in this area of my life, what action would I be taking?

....

....

....

....

....

....

....

....

....

....

....

....

....

....

....

....

....

....

BOX 9

> I commit 100% to this area of my life.
> I know that I count and I act as if I do.

If I really counted in this area of my life, what action would
I be taking?

....

....

....

....

....

....

....

....

....

....

....

....

....

....

....

....

....

....

When I was first shown your book, I had just been admitted to a psychiatric unit suffering from acute anxiety – including agoraphobia. I'm not going to tell you the whole story, sufficient to say that your book gave me practical, positive advice at a time when I wasn't able to make even simple decisions about my future. I made a Pain-to-Power chart in therapy classes (I still have it) and started at the P of pain. I'm now at the P of power. The nine-box grid was immensely helpful also.

When I was first released from hospital I made myself drive the twenty miles to the nearest city. I was absolutely terrified but I had a postcard on the dashboard with 'FEEL THE FEAR AND DO IT ANYWAY' written on it in big red letters. This kept me going when I desperately wanted to turn back. That was six months ago and yesterday I came back from a round trip of 600 miles.

J. P.
Perth, Australia

11

OPEN YOUR EYES TO ABUNDANCE

How good are you at noticing the abundance in your life? Let's test it out. Right now, write *fifty* things for which you are truly grateful. 'How many, Susan? I can't think of five!' I'll give you a hint as to how to get those numbers up: THE ART OF GRATITUDE IS BEING ABLE TO MAKE ORDINARY THINGS IN YOUR LIFE EXTRAORDINARY. Go ahead. Try it!

1.
2.
3.
4.
5.
6.
7.
8.
9.
10.
11.
12.
13.
14.
15.
16.
17.
18.
19.
20.
21.

22.

23.

24.

25.

You're half-way there. Keep going.

26.

27.

28.

29.

30.

31.

32.

33.

34.

35.

36.

37.

38.

39.

40.

41.

42.

43.

44.

Come on . . . you're almost there!

45.

46.

47.

48.

49.

50.

How many wonderful things did you find? One? Fifty? Or somewhere in between? I love giving this assignment in my workshops. I allow five minutes for the list to be completed. It's astounding how varied are the responses. Most of my students are in the 'somewhere in between' category. Sometimes one person finds fifty things to be grateful for, and sometimes one person finds only one thing to be grateful for. Now, whose life do you think feels richer? The student who found one wonderful thing to be grateful for or the student who found fifty? By definition:

THE MORE AWARE YOU ARE OF THE BEAUTY IN YOUR LIFE, THE MORE BEAUTIFUL YOUR LIFE WILL FEEL.

You may be thinking that the person who found fifty items to be grateful for just has a 'better' life materially than the one who only found one. My work with the poor has shown me that you can have very little in terms of material things, but a mountain of wealth when it comes to appreciating the gifts that lie before you every minute of every day. In fact, some of the 'poorest' people I know, in terms of feeling grateful, have an immense amount of money. They have no appreciation of the gifts in their life and so live with a scarcity mentality.

You might be saying to me, 'Susan, you don't know what's going on in my life. It's a mess . . . no abundance here.' I guarantee you that despite what is going on in your life, abundance surrounds you. I have known people with terminal illnesses, who have no money, who are getting a divorce, who have lost a child, and on and on and on – yet they have been very aware of the beauty and blessing in their lives. This awareness of the abundance keeps them in a state of gratitude, even when potentially devastating situations surround them.

In truth, each and every one of us, no matter what our circumstances, could have found fifty things for which to be grateful, that is, IF WE WERE TRAINED TO SEE THE ABUNDANCE IN OUR LIVES – and it is a training. It is also a choice.

Most of us have been trained to see only the scarcity. Just listen to the complaining that goes on within and around you. We definitely live in what I call a 'moan and groan' society. And it is up to each and every one of us to train ourselves to stop complaining and look at the beauty that surrounds us every moment of every day, despite what is happening to us. When we do that, life is not about the scary feeling of 'not enough', it is about the fear-less feeling of abundance.

I've noticed that when I am truly noticing the beauty in my day, the outcome of events in my life doesn't seem so important. Hence, it takes away a lot of my worry. I ask myself, 'Is it really so important how this or that will turn out? No, my life is wonderful.' Your life is wonderful, too.

Now go back to your fifty items if you weren't able to complete the list. And let me help you out. As I hinted in the beginning of this chapter, don't think in terms of the grand splashes of brilliance. When you make the ordinary extraordinary, you bring magic into your life. What ordinary things in your life are extraordinary? Here are some possibilities:

1. You're healthy.
2. You have clothes to keep you warm.
3. Your car started.
4. You have enough food.
5. You have some beautiful flowers in your garden.
6. It is a beautiful day.
7. You had a wonderful hot shower.
8. Your friend called.
9. Your heart is beating.
10. You have an opportunity to warm the world with your love.

And on and on and on. You may feel that beautiful weather has nothing to do with your life. What a gift you are missing! When you grasp the exquisiteness of a warm sunny day, something deeper than your skin is warmed. Your soul is warmed by the awareness of the multitude of things there are in the world that support you. If you don't take in the beauty of ALL the richness around you, you have lost so much, indeed!

Important Tip: I suggest you go out to the store today and buy yourself a notebook or one of those wonderfully decorative empty books now available in many office supply stores and make it your Book of Abundance. It will become a book you will treasure because its contents are the treasures of your life.

One of my students told me he carries a tiny notepad throughout the day to write his blessings as he sees them. In that way, he focuses on the wonder of the day, ALL DAY. And when it comes time to fill in his 'official' Book of Abundance, he just transposes all he has recorded in his notepad. I suggest you do the same thing.

Think about this: when you commit to making your Book of Abundance a daily ritual, you will walk around *looking for* the abundance in your life rather than focusing on what's wrong. Think how your life will be improved when you find yourself truly seeing the beauty in your life, perhaps for the first time.

I've been asked, 'Can I repeat items each day?' Yes, you can. The more you acknowledge the abundance of one particular thing in your life, the more it will become a part of your 'being' of appreciation. I've mentioned the flowers in my courtyard so many times in my Book of Abundance that I can't help but focus on their beauty every time I walk by. There was a time when I would have simply walked by the beauty without noticing. I was too busy focusing on the 'scarcity' of my life, on what I didn't have. As I have already told you, after my experience with cancer, I really have awakened to the beauty that surrounds me every day of my life.

I *implore* you to learn how to pay attention to the joys inherent in your everyday experiences, the joys you are missing when you walk on by the wonders in your life. When you understand this concept, you will never look at the world in the same old mundane, boring way. The world becomes a place of enchantment. Yes, even the traffic jams, screaming children, difficulty at work, and on and on and on, can become part of the grand abundance of life.[10]

I've been searching for such an inspiring book. At the age of 67, you've made me really aware how great my life has been, and how much there is ahead of me. And, particularly, what I am aware of now is that even the difficult times, the mistakes and the total richness of my experiences are what I am all about. They have all been learning experiences and have combined to make my days what they are today, the most rewarding time of my life.

My father-in-law, who just died at the age of 101 years and 3 months, was asked, 'Of all the times that you have lived through, what was the best time for you?' And he replied, 'Today.'

F. W.
Cape Town, South Africa

12

GIVE IT AWAY

I believe that one wonderfully powerful way to decrease your fear is to become a Giver! Why? Because *when your focus is on giving you are not so worried about what you are going to get!*

Right now you may be thinking to yourself, 'I give and give and give. How much can I give?' But: do you give, or do you simply exchange? Are you operating on a barter system? Do you give without expectation of something coming back to you? 'I give this to you but I expect you to give this to me.' As you learn the concept of giving it away, you will be very surprised at how different your perspective of the world will be.

Now don't get frightened that I am asking you to become a doormat for other people to walk upon. You may know my philosophy about that: *there's nothing as unattractive as footprints on the face!* No, I'm talking about an attitude of meaning. I'm talking about seeing yourself as a person who has much to give to this world instead of a whining child complaining that the world is not giving you enough. I'm talking about pulling up your power and love and spreading it into this very needy world.

The key is to be other-involved instead of self-involved. Self-involvement inevitably creates a 'scarcity mentality'. Yes, the same scarcity mentality that is created when one doesn't appreciate all the beauty in one's life. Again, some of the wealthiest people I know are incredibly self-involved and have an intense scarcity mentality. They are always worried about what they are going to get. Yet some of the poorest people I know have an abundance mentality. Not only do they appreciate the beauty in their lives, they are also other-involved. They are focused on the giving of themselves in some way.

When I worked with the poor in New York City, I was always amazed at their capacity for giving, which may have accounted for their cheerful attitude. They cooked at their church kitchens for those who had nothing to eat; they helped in the schools; they were involved in cleaning up their community of drugs. They taught me that the more we move towards being other-involved, the less fear we experience in our daily lives. They are action-oriented. They are involved. They are very powerful people indeed!

Some of you may remember the story I have told about a woman who became ill and was confined to her bed. What did she have to give? So much! She got a list of names from a city agency of others who were also bedridden. She began the practice of calling some of these people every day just to let them know that somebody cared. Instead of lying in her bed bemoaning her condition, she adopted an attitude of giving and made herself and many others very happy!

How do we translate this into our everyday lives? Let me give you an example: I have seen so many 'getters' in the workplace. They worry about how much money they are making and how their boss and other workers treat them, and on and on and on. As I reported in *Dare to Connect*, I had a student like this in one of my classes. Peggy was miserable at her job and couldn't wait to find another one. Nothing was right.

I instructed her to put a sign on her desk for one week that said, 'If I were really important here, what would I be doing?' and participate full-out in doing it. I told her that, even if she didn't feel important in her job, she should 'act-as-if' her actions really made a difference to everyone around them. You will recognize this as the same question you ask yourself as you create your Grid of Life.

Peggy tried it for one week. You would not have believed it was the same person entering the classroom the following session. She radiated joyous energy and a big smile was planted on her face. She couldn't wait to report the events of the previous week:

'My first step was to brighten up the dismal office with some plants and posters. I then started to really pay attention to the people I work with. If someone seemed unhappy, I asked if there was anything wrong and if I could help. If I went out for coffee, I always asked if there was anything I could bring back for the others. I complimented people. I invited two people for lunch. I told the boss something wonderful about one of my co-workers. (Usually I'm selling myself!)

Then I asked myself how I could improve things for the company itself. First I stopped complaining about the job – I realized I was such a nag! I became a self-starter and came up with a few very good ideas which I began implementing. Every day I made a list of things I wanted to accomplish and I set about accomplishing them. I was really surprised by how much I could do in a day when I focused on what I was doing! I also noticed how fast the day goes by when I am involved. I put a sign on my desk that said, "If I were really important here, what would I be doing?" And every time I started to fall back into my old patterns of boredom and complaining, the sign reminded me what I was supposed to be doing. That really helped.'

This is only a shortened version of her enthusiastic report, but you get the picture. By acting as if she were really important and giving, she created a 'new' job – one filled with excitement, joy, caring, comfort and all good things.

It's important to note that her commitment didn't mean

she had to stay at this job forever; it only meant that, while she was there, it was in everyone's best interest, particularly her own, to create a caring environment. Who wants to spend their days in an energy filled with alienation, boredom and negativity? (I would find it strange if anyone answered 'I do!' to that question!) It is also worth noting that with such positive energy, the likelihood of Peggy getting a great recommendation and finding a new, more challenging job would be greatly increased!

Peggy learned how to 'give it away'. It's time to look at your own life and determine how you are going to 'give it away', whatever that means to you. I've created four areas where you can practise 'giving it away'. Fill in the following, being as creative as you can be:

Time: To whom will you give your time? List five ways you can give your time to those who need it.

1. ....

2. ....

3. ....

4. ....

5. ....

Money: To whom will you give your money? List five ways you can give your money to those who need it.

1. ....

2. ....

3. ....

4. ....

5. ....

Praise: To whom will you give your praise? List five people you will praise for their contribution to your life or to this world.

1. ....

2. ....

3. ....

4. ....

5. ....

Thanks: To whom will you give your thanks? Each day people contribute to your world. Who will you thank?

1. ....

2. ....

3. ....

4. ....

5. ....

Now your task is to begin 'giving it away', using the above list as a start. Understand that giving it away has to be a meaningful part of your everyday life so remember to include acts of giving in your 'action lists' for your Fear-Less Grid of Life (pages 116–133). Ultimately, your spiritual journey asks that you transform yourself from a needy, taking child to an abundant, giving adult. When you become the latter, instead of always worrying about what you are going to get, fear fades into the background. Instead, abundance fills your life. How fortunate we all are to be able to take this magical journey from the pain of neediness to the power of abundance.

I feel more in control of my life now than at any time previously – and much of it I owe to the advice and encouragement of your book, Feel the Fear and Do It Anyway. *I have applied the 'whole life' approach you recommended and my life is fuller and richer for it. I now feel like a strong table with eight or more legs, so that I know that if one or two were cut off, I would still be stable and capable of supporting myself! Before, I felt like a table with only two shaky legs: job and relationship.*

I have gone back to college; I help produce a 'talking newspaper' for the blind and am also involved with helping handicapped people in their daily lives. I go skiing once a week on a nearby slope and have widened my circle of acquaintances. I have also made one or two new close friends, which I regard as a major achievement.

I think you can tell from the above that I have made a good start and am feeling optimistic about my life. Much of this I owe to your good advice and the 'push' to hold my fear and do it anyway!

V. S.
Birmingham, UK

PART V

There's Always More

There you have it. A dozen powerful Higher-Self tools to dip into when the Lower Self takes over and, for all of us, this is a very frequent occurrence! But when the tools are imprinted in your being, spiritual help is always at hand. Here are a few important points to notice:

1. When things are improving there is a tendency to stop doing the exercises. The world won't come to an end if you do stop, of course, but you will lose the feeling of power and love that you worked so hard to achieve.

2. Don't punish yourself if you do get off the path once in a while. Just notice when you do and start using the exercises as soon as possible.

3. A failure to do the exercises often comes from pure forgetfulness. Surround yourself with reminders. If you don't, fear will creep in when you aren't even looking.

4. A failure to do the exercises also often comes from our tendency to sabotage ourselves in some way. Remember that change itself can be uncomfortable and often frightening. Progress occurs when we push through the discomfort.

5. Keep renewing your commitment to the exercises. Think of them as food for the mind. Without 'eating' regularly we starve, spiritually speaking.

6. Always be patient with yourself! It takes time to cultivate the power and love we hold inside. Sometimes we don't realize that change is occurring but, when doing the exercises, it truly is. All that's right will happen in its own time. One day the fruits of your learning will erupt into a wonderful display of power and love. Yes, all in its own right time.

7. Remember, there is always more. While the tools in this book will take you a long way, I also suggest you explore the tools in my other self-help books and those of other writers', including tapes and workshops. The world is filled with spiritual gold! Go for it! Explore it all! You have a whole life to practise FEELING THE FEAR AND DOING IT ANYWAY. Oh, yes – and I'll be right there with you. We're all in this together!

PART VI

30-Day
'Power Planner'

Each year more and more daily planners and diaries line our bookshop shelves. Most of us use these items to remember business activities for the day. Once in a while an appointment for the dentist is noted or dinner plans with friends but there is much more our daily planner needs to include to remind us of the richness of our lives as well as the huge amount of power and love we hold inside.

What follows is my '30-Day Power Planner' which encompasses many of the things I've talked about in this book: affirmations, the Magic Duo, the risk of the day, the Grid of Life, the Pain-to-Power chart, gratitude, and more. The Power Planner is a tool that is designed to be used *after* you have completed the other exercises in this book.

I've had a lot of fun creating this daily planner for you, and for me. I hope it gives you a wonderful framework for creating a rich and beautiful life. If you find it helpful, don't stop there. Create your own Power Planner for the rest of the year!

Before you begin using it, however, let me give you a few helpful instructions:

1. Begin each day by reading the 'Statement Of Intention'. The DAILY repetition of this will help plant it solidly in your mind. Read it *consciously* with the ultimate goal of memorizing it. Not only will it set the tone for all that you do during the day, it will also remind you of all the power and love you hold inside: a Higher-Self message indeed.

2. If the affirmation I've provided doesn't intuitively feel right for you on any particular day, write in a new one that

has more relevance for what is happening in your life. You might want to place your daily affirmations around on index cards wherever you can see them.

3. I have included nine sections to represent your Grid of Life. If yours contains different categories, simply write over the ones I've provided or write a new category in the 'Other' section. Refer back to the actions you've created for your Grid of Life on pages 125–133 and include them, one by one, in your daily activities throughout the 30-day period.

4. You'll notice I have left more room in the area of 'Work'. This is not because it is more important than the rest but because the other categories will most likely have fewer items on any given day.

5. The area of 'Work' also includes that of homemaker which, after all, is a career in its own right.

6. I've included a 'Gratitude' section. It is important that as you go through the day you notice the beauty all around you. You can transfer these items into your Book of Abundance at the end of the day.

7. I've included the 'Risk of the Day' to help you expand your Comfort Zone. Remember: these risks do not include physically dangerous acts or any acts that hurt other people. It is a life-affirming risk that you are going to take.

8. Each day has a Pain-to-Power chart. Choose a personalized way of marking the place where you see yourself on this at the end of each particular day. Hopefully, as the month goes by, your sense of power and love will increase. If it doesn't, perhaps you are judging yourself too harshly instead of patting yourself on the back for the work you are doing! Remember, patting yourself on the back is a very important part of feeling powerful and loving!

9. Perhaps the most important thing I can tell you about the daily planner is DON'T GET COMPULSIVE ABOUT IT! There are times when you will be restricted to only a few items in your Grid because of a special project at work, or

family considerations or ill health. This is to be expected. So don't drive yourself crazy lamenting you are not building a rich life. This will simply create more pain. Even if you don't fill in all the boxes in a given day, they will be there as a constant reminder of the beauty in your life. Remember, your goal is to create an attitude of fullness and action for a beautiful life.

My hope is that such a planner will help you enjoy your life in a much more conscious, loving, giving and powerful way. As I told you earlier, LIFE IS HUGE! Enjoy it all!

30-DAY
POWER PLANNER

SAMPLE DAY OF POWER AND LOVE

Day 1 Affirmation

I am powerful and I am loving and I have nothing to fear . . .

> I commit 100% to each area of my life.
> I know that I count and I act as if I do.

MY LIFE IS RICH

SPIRITUAL GROWTH *Do my affirmations for 20 minutes through-out the day*

RELATIONSHIP *Send Mike some flowers*

FAMILY *Call Aunt Alice*

FRIENDS *Invite Betty to lunch*

PERSONAL GROWTH *Go to my French class*

ALONE TIME *Take a long, hot bath*

CONTRIBUTION TO THE COMMUNITY *Send some clothes to the Homeless Shelter*

PLAYTIME *Meet Carole for a snack after work*

WORK *Work on the proposal for the Sacks account. Call Bob Myers to see if he got my package. Come up with a new idea for the Grant account. Thank Jane for being such a caring boss. Buy some cookies for the office.*

RISK OF THE DAY *Sending Mike flowers is a big risk!*

TODAY I AM GRATEFUL FOR *My health, the beautiful weather, my family and friends, my wonderful job . . . and Mike*

Where do I stand on my Pain-to-Power chart?

PAIN ☆ POWER

SO TO BEGIN . . .

DAY 1
STATEMENT OF INTENTION

I am now tuning in to the best of who I am: the part of me that is loving, giving, confident, appreciative, peaceful and patient. I open my heart and allow loving energy to flow through me. I am aware that my life makes a difference and that every action I take helps to heal the hurts within and around me.

I move into life knowing there is nothing to fear. Within me is an endless source of wisdom and strength that will handle all that needs to be handled. I am being shown the way. I move into the light and see the huge expanse of possibility. Today I push away all self-doubt and replace it with self-trust. I constantly remind myself my life is unfolding in a perfect way. I trust the Grand Design.

I am grateful for the opportunity to create love in this world. I am listening to the Divine within me. I appreciate all the opportunities this life gives me for becoming a more caring and compassionate human being. I am truly blessed.

Day 1 Affirmation

I am powerful and I am loving and I have nothing to fear . . .

> I commit 100% to each area of my life.
> I know that I count and I act as if I do.

MY LIFE IS RICH

SPIRITUAL GROWTH
....

RELATIONSHIP
....

FAMILY
....

FRIENDS
....

PERSONAL GROWTH
....

ALONE TIME
....

CONTRIBUTION TO THE COMMUNITY
....

PLAYTIME
....

WORK

....

(OTHER)
....

RISK OF THE DAY
....

TODAY I AM GRATEFUL FOR

....

Where do I stand on my Pain-to-Power chart?

PAIN   POWER

DAY 2
STATEMENT OF INTENTION

I am now tuning in to the best of who I am: the part of me that is loving, giving, confident, appreciative, peaceful and patient. I open my heart and allow loving energy to flow through me. I am aware that my life makes a difference and that every action I take helps to heal the hurts within and around me.

I move into life knowing there is nothing to fear. Within me is an endless source of wisdom and strength that will handle all that needs to be handled. I am being shown the way. I move into the light and see the huge expanse of possibility. Today I push away all self-doubt and replace it with self-trust. I constantly remind myself my life is unfolding in a perfect way. I trust the Grand Design.

I am grateful for the opportunity to create love in this world. I am listening to the Divine within me. I appreciate all the opportunities this life gives me for becoming a more caring and compassionate human being. I am truly blessed.

Day 2 Affirmation

I act responsibly and lovingly toward myself and others.

> I commit 100% to each area of my life.
> I know that I count and I act as if I do.

MY LIFE IS RICH

SPIRITUAL GROWTH
....

RELATIONSHIP
....

FAMILY
....

FRIENDS
....

PERSONAL GROWTH
....

ALONE TIME
....

CONTRIBUTION TO THE COMMUNITY
....

PLAYTIME
....

WORK
....

(OTHER)
....

RISK OF THE DAY
....

TODAY I AM GRATEFUL FOR
....

Where do I stand on my Pain-to-Power chart?

▶ ▶ ▶ ▶ ▶ ▶ ▶ ▶ ▶ ▶ ▶ ▶ ▶ ▶ ▶ ▶ ▶ ▶ ▶ ▶

PAIN   **POWER**

I am now tuning in to the best of who I am: the part of me that is loving, giving, confident, appreciative, peaceful and patient. I open my heart and allow loving energy to flow through me. I am aware that my life makes a difference and that every action I take helps to heal the hurts within and around me.

I move into life knowing there is nothing to fear. Within me is an endless source of wisdom and strength that will handle all that needs to be handled. I am being shown the way. I move into the light and see the huge expanse of possibility. Today I push away all self-doubt and replace it with self-trust. I constantly remind myself my life is unfolding in a perfect way. I trust the Grand Design.

I am grateful for the opportunity to create love in this world. I am listening to the Divine within me. I appreciate all the opportunities this life gives me for becoming a more caring and compassionate human being. I am truly blessed.

Day 3 Affirmation

I keep my heart open to receive all the riches before me.

> I commit 100% to each area of my life.
> I know that I count and I act as if I do.

MY LIFE IS RICH

SPIRITUAL GROWTH
....

RELATIONSHIP
....

FAMILY
....

FRIENDS
....

PERSONAL GROWTH
....

ALONE TIME
....

CONTRIBUTION TO THE COMMUNITY
....

PLAYTIME
....

WORK

....

(OTHER)
....

RISK OF THE DAY
....

TODAY I AM GRATEFUL FOR

....

Where do I stand on my Pain-to-Power chart?

PAIN   POWER

I am now tuning in to the best of who I am: the part of me that is loving, giving, confident, appreciative, peaceful and patient. I open my heart and allow loving energy to flow through me. I am aware that my life makes a difference and that every action I take helps to heal the hurts within and around me.

I move into life knowing there is nothing to fear. Within me is an endless source of wisdom and strength that will handle all that needs to be handled. I am being shown the way. I move into the light and see the huge expanse of possibility. Today I push away all self-doubt and replace it with self-trust. I constantly remind myself my life is unfolding in a perfect way. I trust the Grand Design.

I am grateful for the opportunity to create love in this world. I am listening to the Divine within me. I appreciate all the opportunities this life gives me for becoming a more caring and compassionate human being. I am truly blessed.

Day 4 Affirmation

I am sculpting my life the way I want it to be.

> I commit 100% to each area of my life.
> I know that I count and I act as if I do.

MY LIFE IS RICH

SPIRITUAL GROWTH
....

RELATIONSHIP
....

FAMILY
....

FRIENDS
....

PERSONAL GROWTH
....

ALONE TIME
....

CONTRIBUTION TO THE COMMUNITY
....

PLAYTIME
....

WORK

....

(OTHER)
....

RISK OF THE DAY
....

TODAY I AM GRATEFUL FOR

....

Where do I stand on my Pain-to-Power chart?

PAIN   POWER

I am now tuning in to the best of who I am: the part of me that is loving, giving, confident, appreciative, peaceful and patient. I open my heart and allow loving energy to flow through me. I am aware that my life makes a difference and that every action I take helps to heal the hurts within and around me.

I move into life knowing there is nothing to fear. Within me is an endless source of wisdom and strength that will handle all that needs to be handled. I am being shown the way. I move into the light and see the huge expanse of possibility. Today I push away all self-doubt and replace it with self-trust. I constantly remind myself my life is unfolding in a perfect way. I trust the Grand Design.

I am grateful for the opportunity to create love in this world. I am listening to the Divine within me. I appreciate all the opportunities this life gives me for becoming a more caring and compassionate human being. I am truly blessed.

Day 5 Affirmation

I release my fear about the outcome of all situations in my life.

> I commit 100% to each area of my life.
> I know that I count and I act as if I do.

MY LIFE IS RICH

SPIRITUAL GROWTH
....

RELATIONSHIP
....

FAMILY
....

FRIENDS
....

PERSONAL GROWTH
....

ALONE TIME
....

CONTRIBUTION TO THE COMMUNITY
....

PLAYTIME
....

WORK

....

(OTHER)
....

RISK OF THE DAY
....

TODAY I AM GRATEFUL FOR

....

Where do I stand on my Pain-to-Power chart?

PAIN   POWER

am now tuning in to the best of who I am: the part of me that is loving, giving, confident, appreciative, peaceful and patient. I open my heart and allow loving energy to flow through me. I am aware that my life makes a difference and that every action I take helps to heal the hurts within and around me.

I move into life knowing there is nothing to fear. Within me is an endless source of wisdom and strength that will handle all that needs to be handled. I am being shown the way. I move into the light and see the huge expanse of possibility. Today I push away all self-doubt and replace it with self-trust. I constantly remind myself my life is unfolding in a perfect way. I trust the Grand Design.

I am grateful for the opportunity to create love in this world. I am listening to the Divine within me. I appreciate all the opportunities this life gives me for becoming a more caring and compassionate human being. I am truly blessed.

Day 6 Affirmation

I let go and trust that my life is happening perfectly.

> I commit 100% to each area of my life.
> I know that I count and I act as if I do.

MY LIFE IS RICH

SPIRITUAL GROWTH
....

RELATIONSHIP
....

FAMILY
....

FRIENDS
....

PERSONAL GROWTH
....

ALONE TIME
....

CONTRIBUTION TO THE COMMUNITY
....

PLAYTIME
....

WORK
....

....

(OTHER)
....

RISK OF THE DAY
....

TODAY I AM GRATEFUL FOR

....

Where do I stand on my Pain-to-Power chart?

▶ ▶ ▶ ▶ ▶ ▶ ▶ ▶ ▶ ▶ ▶ ▶ ▶ ▶ ▶ ▶ ▶ ▶ ▶

PAIN   **POWER**

I am now tuning in to the best of who I am: the part of me that is loving, giving, confident, appreciative, peaceful and patient. I open my heart and allow loving energy to flow through me. I am aware that my life makes a difference and that every action I take helps to heal the hurts within and around me.

I move into life knowing there is nothing to fear. Within me is an endless source of wisdom and strength that will handle all that needs to be handled. I am being shown the way. I move into the light and see the huge expanse of possibility. Today I push away all self-doubt and replace it with self-trust. I constantly remind myself my life is unfolding in a perfect way. I trust the Grand Design.

I am grateful for the opportunity to create love in this world. I am listening to the Divine within me. I appreciate all the opportunities this life gives me for becoming a more caring and compassionate human being. I am truly blessed.

Day 7 Affirmation

Love is my life and I put love into everything I do.

> I commit 100% to each area of my life.
> I know that I count and I act as if I do.

MY LIFE IS RICH

SPIRITUAL GROWTH
....

RELATIONSHIP
....

FAMILY
....

FRIENDS
....

PERSONAL GROWTH
....

ALONE TIME
....

CONTRIBUTION TO THE COMMUNITY
....

PLAYTIME
....

WORK
....

....

(OTHER)
....

RISK OF THE DAY
....

TODAY I AM GRATEFUL FOR

....

Where do I stand on my Pain-to-Power chart?

PAIN   **POWER**

DAY 8
STATEMENT OF INTENTION

I am now tuning in to the best of who I am: the part of me that is loving, giving, confident, appreciative, peaceful and patient. I open my heart and allow loving energy to flow through me. I am aware that my life makes a difference and that every action I take helps to heal the hurts within and around me.

I move into life knowing there is nothing to fear. Within me is an endless source of wisdom and strength that will handle all that needs to be handled. I am being shown the way. I move into the light and see the huge expanse of possibility. Today I push away all self-doubt and replace it with self-trust. I constantly remind myself my life is unfolding in a perfect way. I trust the Grand Design.

I am grateful for the opportunity to create love in this world. I am listening to the Divine within me. I appreciate all the opportunities this life gives me for becoming a more caring and compassionate human being. I am truly blessed.

Day 8 Affirmation

I always choose the path with the heart.

> I commit 100% to each area of my life.
> I know that I count and I act as if I do.

MY LIFE IS RICH

SPIRITUAL GROWTH
....
RELATIONSHIP
....
FAMILY
....
FRIENDS
....
PERSONAL GROWTH
....
ALONE TIME
....
CONTRIBUTION TO THE COMMUNITY
....
PLAYTIME
....
WORK
....

....
(OTHER)
....
RISK OF THE DAY
....
TODAY I AM GRATEFUL FOR

....

Where do I stand on my Pain-to-Power chart?

▶ ▶ ▶ ▶ ▶ ▶ ▶ ▶ ▶ ▶ ▶ ▶ ▶ ▶ ▶ ▶ ▶ ▶ ▶ ▶

PAIN   **POWER**

I am now tuning in to the best of who I am: the part of me that is loving, giving, confident, appreciative, peaceful and patient. I open my heart and allow loving energy to flow through me. I am aware that my life makes a difference and that every action I take helps to heal the hurts within and around me.

I move into life knowing there is nothing to fear. Within me is an endless source of wisdom and strength that will handle all that needs to be handled. I am being shown the way. I move into the light and see the huge expanse of possibility. Today I push away all self-doubt and replace it with self-trust. I constantly remind myself my life is unfolding in a perfect way. I trust the Grand Design.

I am grateful for the opportunity to create love in this world. I am listening to the Divine within me. I appreciate all the opportunities this life gives me for becoming a more caring and compassionate human being. I am truly blessed.

Day 9 Affirmation

I am finding a solution to all tasks placed before me.

> I commit 100% to each area of my life.
> I know that I count and I act as if I do.

MY LIFE IS RICH

SPIRITUAL GROWTH
....
RELATIONSHIP
....
FAMILY
....
FRIENDS
....
PERSONAL GROWTH
....
ALONE TIME
....
CONTRIBUTION TO THE COMMUNITY
....
PLAYTIME
....
WORK

....
(OTHER)
....
RISK OF THE DAY
....
TODAY I AM GRATEFUL FOR

....

Where do I stand on my Pain-to-Power chart?

PAIN   POWER

I am now tuning in to the best of who I am: the part of me that is loving, giving, confident, appreciative, peaceful and patient. I open my heart and allow loving energy to flow through me. I am aware that my life makes a difference and that every action I take helps to heal the hurts within and around me.

I move into life knowing there is nothing to fear. Within me is an endless source of wisdom and strength that will handle all that needs to be handled. I am being shown the way. I move into the light and see the huge expanse of possibility. Today I push away all self-doubt and replace it with self-trust. I constantly remind myself my life is unfolding in a perfect way. I trust the Grand Design.

I am grateful for the opportunity to create love in this world. I am listening to the Divine within me. I appreciate all the opportunities this life gives me for becoming a more caring and compassionate human being. I am truly blessed.

Day 10 Affirmation

I feel the power and love that my soul radiates.

> I commit 100% to each area of my life.
> I know that I count and I act as if I do.

MY LIFE IS RICH

SPIRITUAL GROWTH
....
RELATIONSHIP
....
FAMILY
....
FRIENDS
....
PERSONAL GROWTH
....
ALONE TIME
....
CONTRIBUTION TO THE COMMUNITY
....
PLAYTIME
....
WORK

....
(OTHER)
....
RISK OF THE DAY
....
TODAY I AM GRATEFUL FOR

....

Where do I stand on my Pain-to-Power chart?

▶ ▶ ▶ ▶ ▶ ▶ ▶ ▶ ▶ ▶ ▶ ▶ ▶ ▶ ▶ ▶ ▶ ▶ ▶ ▶

PAIN   **POWER**

DAY 11
STATEMENT OF INTENTION

I am now tuning in to the best of who I am: the part of me that is loving, giving, confident, appreciative, peaceful and patient. I open my heart and allow loving energy to flow through me. I am aware that my life makes a difference and that every action I take helps to heal the hurts within and around me.

I move into life knowing there is nothing to fear. Within me is an endless source of wisdom and strength that will handle all that needs to be handled. I am being shown the way. I move into the light and see the huge expanse of possibility. Today I push away all self-doubt and replace it with self-trust. I constantly remind myself my life is unfolding in a perfect way. I trust the Grand Design.

I am grateful for the opportunity to create love in this world. I am listening to the Divine within me. I appreciate all the opportunities this life gives me for becoming a more caring and compassionate human being. I am truly blessed.

Day 11 Affirmation

I relax knowing I can handle all that needs to be handled.

I commit 100% to each area of my life.
I know that I count and I act as if I do.

MY LIFE IS RICH

SPIRITUAL GROWTH
....
RELATIONSHIP
....
FAMILY
....
FRIENDS
....
PERSONAL GROWTH
....
ALONE TIME
....
CONTRIBUTION TO THE COMMUNITY
....
PLAYTIME
....
WORK

....
(OTHER)
....
RISK OF THE DAY
....
TODAY I AM GRATEFUL FOR

....

Where do I stand on my Pain-to-Power chart?

PAIN   POWER

I am now tuning in to the best of who I am: the part of me that is loving, giving, confident, appreciative, peaceful and patient. I open my heart and allow loving energy to flow through me. I am aware that my life makes a difference and that every action I take helps to heal the hurts within and around me.

I move into life knowing there is nothing to fear. Within me is an endless source of wisdom and strength that will handle all that needs to be handled. I am being shown the way. I move into the light and see the huge expanse of possibility. Today I push away all self-doubt and replace it with self-trust. I constantly remind myself my life is unfolding in a perfect way. I trust the Grand Design.

I am grateful for the opportunity to create love in this world. I am listening to the Divine within me. I appreciate all the opportunities this life gives me for becoming a more caring and compassionate human being. I am truly blessed.

Day 12 Affirmation

My life is happening perfectly for my Highest good.

> I commit 100% to each area of my life.
> I know that I count and I act as if I do.

MY LIFE IS RICH

SPIRITUAL GROWTH
....

RELATIONSHIP
....

FAMILY
....

FRIENDS
....

PERSONAL GROWTH
....

ALONE TIME
....

CONTRIBUTION TO THE COMMUNITY
....

PLAYTIME
....

WORK

....

(OTHER)
....

RISK OF THE DAY
....

TODAY I AM GRATEFUL FOR

....

Where do I stand on my Pain-to-Power chart?

PAIN   **POWER**

I am now tuning in to the best of who I am: the part of me that is loving, giving, confident, appreciative, peaceful and patient. I open my heart and allow loving energy to flow through me. I am aware that my life makes a difference and that every action I take helps to heal the hurts within and around me.

I move into life knowing there is nothing to fear. Within me is an endless source of wisdom and strength that will handle all that needs to be handled. I am being shown the way. I move into the light and see the huge expanse of possibility. Today I push away all self-doubt and replace it with self-trust. I constantly remind myself my life is unfolding in a perfect way. I trust the Grand Design.

I am grateful for the opportunity to create love in this world. I am listening to the Divine within me. I appreciate all the opportunities this life gives me for becoming a more caring and compassionate human being. I am truly blessed.

Day 13 Affirmation

I am creating a rich and joyful life . . . one step at a time.

> I commit 100% to each area of my life.
> I know that I count and I act as if I do.

MY LIFE IS RICH

SPIRITUAL GROWTH
....

RELATIONSHIP
....

FAMILY
....

FRIENDS
....

PERSONAL GROWTH
....

ALONE TIME
....

CONTRIBUTION TO THE COMMUNITY
....

PLAYTIME
....

WORK

....

(OTHER)
....

RISK OF THE DAY
....

TODAY I AM GRATEFUL FOR

....

Where do I stand on my Pain-to-Power chart?

PAIN   **POWER**

I am now tuning in to the best of who I am: the part of me that is loving, giving, confident, appreciative, peaceful and patient. I open my heart and allow loving energy to flow through me. I am aware that my life makes a difference and that every action I take helps to heal the hurts within and around me.

I move into life knowing there is nothing to fear. Within me is an endless source of wisdom and strength that will handle all that needs to be handled. I am being shown the way. I move into the light and see the huge expanse of possibility. Today I push away all self-doubt and replace it with self-trust. I constantly remind myself my life is unfolding in a perfect way. I trust the Grand Design.

I am grateful for the opportunity to create love in this world. I am listening to the Divine within me. I appreciate all the opportunities this life gives me for becoming a more caring and compassionate human being. I am truly blessed.

Day 14 Affirmation

I let go and let the river carry me to new adventures.

> I commit 100% to each area of my life.
> I know that I count and I act as if I do.

MY LIFE IS RICH

SPIRITUAL GROWTH
....

RELATIONSHIP
....

FAMILY
....

FRIENDS
....

PERSONAL GROWTH
....

ALONE TIME
....

CONTRIBUTION TO THE COMMUNITY
....

PLAYTIME
....

WORK

....

(OTHER)
....

RISK OF THE DAY
....

TODAY I AM GRATEFUL FOR

....

Where do I stand on my Pain-to-Power chart?

▶ ▶ ▶ ▶ ▶ ▶ ▶ ▶ ▶ ▶ ▶ ▶ ▶ ▶ ▶ ▶ ▶ ▶ ▶ ▶

PAIN   **POWER**

I am now tuning in to the best of who I am: the part of me that is loving, giving, confident, appreciative, peaceful and patient. I open my heart and allow loving energy to flow through me. I am aware that my life makes a difference and that every action I take helps to heal the hurts within and around me.

I move into life knowing there is nothing to fear. Within me is an endless source of wisdom and strength that will handle all that needs to be handled. I am being shown the way. I move into the light and see the huge expanse of possibility. Today I push away all self-doubt and replace it with self-trust. I constantly remind myself my life is unfolding in a perfect way. I trust the Grand Design.

I am grateful for the opportunity to create love in this world. I am listening to the Divine within me. I appreciate all the opportunities this life gives me for becoming a more caring and compassionate human being. I am truly blessed.

Day 15 Affirmation

The loving arms of my inner light keep me safe.

> I commit 100% to each area of my life.
> I know that I count and I act as if I do.

MY LIFE IS RICH

SPIRITUAL GROWTH
....

RELATIONSHIP
....

FAMILY
....

FRIENDS
....

PERSONAL GROWTH
....

ALONE TIME
....

CONTRIBUTION TO THE COMMUNITY
....

PLAYTIME
....

WORK

....

(OTHER)
....

RISK OF THE DAY
....

TODAY I AM GRATEFUL FOR

....

Where do I stand on my Pain-to-Power chart?

PAIN   POWER

I am now tuning in to the best of who I am: the part of me that is loving, giving, confident, appreciative, peaceful and patient. I open my heart and allow loving energy to flow through me. I am aware that my life makes a difference and that every action I take helps to heal the hurts within and around me.

I move into life knowing there is nothing to fear. Within me is an endless source of wisdom and strength that will handle all that needs to be handled. I am being shown the way. I move into the light and see the huge expanse of possibility. Today I push away all self-doubt and replace it with self-trust. I constantly remind myself my life is unfolding in a perfect way. I trust the Grand Design.

I am grateful for the opportunity to create love in this world. I am listening to the Divine within me. I appreciate all the opportunities this life gives me for becoming a more caring and compassionate human being. I am truly blessed.

Day 16 Affirmation

I put aside all stressful thoughts and focus on what is beautiful now.

I commit 100% to each area of my life.
I know that I count and I act as if I do.

MY LIFE IS RICH

SPIRITUAL GROWTH

RELATIONSHIP

FAMILY

FRIENDS

PERSONAL GROWTH

ALONE TIME

CONTRIBUTION TO THE COMMUNITY

PLAYTIME

WORK

(OTHER)

RISK OF THE DAY

TODAY I AM GRATEFUL FOR

Where do I stand on my Pain-to-Power chart?

PAIN   POWER

DAY 17
STATEMENT OF INTENTION

I am now tuning in to the best of who I am: the part of me that is loving, giving, confident, appreciative, peaceful and patient. I open my heart and allow loving energy to flow through me. I am aware that my life makes a difference and that every action I take helps to heal the hurts within and around me.

I move into life knowing there is nothing to fear. Within me is an endless source of wisdom and strength that will handle all that needs to be handled. I am being shown the way. I move into the light and see the huge expanse of possibility. Today I push away all self-doubt and replace it with self-trust. I constantly remind myself my life is unfolding in a perfect way. I trust the Grand Design.

I am grateful for the opportunity to create love in this world. I am listening to the Divine within me. I appreciate all the opportunities this life gives me for becoming a more caring and compassionate human being. I am truly blessed.

Day 17 Affirmation

Everything I do is perfect for my growth and self-discovery.

> I commit 100% to each area of my life.
> I know that I count and I act as if I do.

MY LIFE IS RICH

SPIRITUAL GROWTH

....

RELATIONSHIP

....

FAMILY

....

FRIENDS

....

PERSONAL GROWTH

....

ALONE TIME

....

CONTRIBUTION TO THE COMMUNITY

....

PLAYTIME

....

WORK

....

....

(OTHER)

....

RISK OF THE DAY

....

TODAY I AM GRATEFUL FOR

....

Where do I stand on my Pain-to-Power chart?

PAIN   POWER

I am now tuning in to the best of who I am: the part of me that is loving, giving, confident, appreciative, peaceful and patient. I open my heart and allow loving energy to flow through me. I am aware that my life makes a difference and that every action I take helps to heal the hurts within and around me.

I move into life knowing there is nothing to fear. Within me is an endless source of wisdom and strength that will handle all that needs to be handled. I am being shown the way. I move into the light and see the huge expanse of possibility. Today I push away all self-doubt and replace it with self-trust. I constantly remind myself my life is unfolding in a perfect way. I trust the Grand Design.

I am grateful for the opportunity to create love in this world. I am listening to the Divine within me. I appreciate all the opportunities this life gives me for becoming a more caring and compassionate human being. I am truly blessed.

Day 18 Affirmation

I am reaching out and inviting others into my life.

> I commit 100% to each area of my life.
> I know that I count and I act as if I do.

MY LIFE IS RICH

SPIRITUAL GROWTH
....

RELATIONSHIP
....

FAMILY
....

FRIENDS
....

PERSONAL GROWTH
....

ALONE TIME
....

CONTRIBUTION TO THE COMMUNITY
....

PLAYTIME
....

WORK
....

(OTHER)
....

RISK OF THE DAY
....

TODAY I AM GRATEFUL FOR
....

Where do I stand on my Pain-to-Power chart?

▶ ▶ ▶ ▶ ▶ ▶ ▶ ▶ ▶ ▶ ▶ ▶ ▶ ▶ ▶ ▶ ▶ ▶ ▶

PAIN   **POWER**

I am now tuning in to the best of who I am: the part of me that is loving, giving, confident, appreciative, peaceful and patient. I open my heart and allow loving energy to flow through me. I am aware that my life makes a difference and that every action I take helps to heal the hurts within and around me.

I move into life knowing there is nothing to fear. Within me is an endless source of wisdom and strength that will handle all that needs to be handled. I am being shown the way. I move into the light and see the huge expanse of possibility. Today I push away all self-doubt and replace it with self-trust. I constantly remind myself my life is unfolding in a perfect way. I trust the Grand Design.

I am grateful for the opportunity to create love in this world. I am listening to the Divine within me. I appreciate all the opportunities this life gives me for becoming a more caring and compassionate human being. I am truly blessed.

Day 19 Affirmation

I am a lover-in-training and I am learning my lessons well.

> I commit 100% to each area of my life.
> I know that I count and I act as if I do.

MY LIFE IS RICH

SPIRITUAL GROWTH
....

RELATIONSHIP
....

FAMILY
....

FRIENDS
....

PERSONAL GROWTH
....

ALONE TIME
....

CONTRIBUTION TO THE COMMUNITY
....

PLAYTIME
....

WORK

....

(OTHER)
....

RISK OF THE DAY
....

TODAY I AM GRATEFUL FOR

....

Where do I stand on my Pain-to-Power chart?

PAIN   POWER

am now tuning in to the best of who I am: the part of me that is loving, giving, confident, appreciative, peaceful and patient. I open my heart and allow loving energy to flow through me. I am aware that my life makes a difference and that every action I take helps to heal the hurts within and around me.

I move into life knowing there is nothing to fear. Within me is an endless source of wisdom and strength that will handle all that needs to be handled. I am being shown the way. I move into the light and see the huge expanse of possibility. Today I push away all self-doubt and replace it with self-trust. I constantly remind myself my life is unfolding in a perfect way. I trust the Grand Design.

I am grateful for the opportunity to create love in this world. I am listening to the Divine within me. I appreciate all the opportunities this life gives me for becoming a more caring and compassionate human being. I am truly blessed.

Day 20 Affirmation

I joyfully thank those who have contributed to my life.

I commit 100% to each area of my life.
I know that I count and I act as if I do.

MY LIFE IS RICH

SPIRITUAL GROWTH

RELATIONSHIP

FAMILY

FRIENDS

PERSONAL GROWTH

ALONE TIME

CONTRIBUTION TO THE COMMUNITY

PLAYTIME

WORK

(OTHER)

RISK OF THE DAY

TODAY I AM GRATEFUL FOR

Where do I stand on my Pain-to-Power chart?

PAIN   POWER

DAY 21
STATEMENT OF INTENTION

I am now tuning in to the best of who I am: the part of me that is loving, giving, confident, appreciative, peaceful and patient. I open my heart and allow loving energy to flow through me. I am aware that my life makes a difference and that every action I take helps to heal the hurts within and around me.

I move into life knowing there is nothing to fear. Within me is an endless source of wisdom and strength that will handle all that needs to be handled. I am being shown the way. I move into the light and see the huge expanse of possibility. Today I push away all self-doubt and replace it with self-trust. I constantly remind myself my life is unfolding in a perfect way. I trust the Grand Design.

I am grateful for the opportunity to create love in this world. I am listening to the Divine within me. I appreciate all the opportunities this life gives me for becoming a more caring and compassionate human being. I am truly blessed.

Day 21 Affirmation

I am learning something valuable from all life's experiences.

> I commit 100% to each area of my life.
> I know that I count and I act as if I do.

MY LIFE IS RICH

SPIRITUAL GROWTH
....
RELATIONSHIP
....
FAMILY
....
FRIENDS
....
PERSONAL GROWTH
....
ALONE TIME
....
CONTRIBUTION TO THE COMMUNITY
....
PLAYTIME
....
WORK

....
(OTHER)
....
RISK OF THE DAY
....
TODAY I AM GRATEFUL FOR

....

Where do I stand on my Pain-to-Power chart?

PAIN　　　　　　　　　　　　　　　　　　　　　　POWER

DAY 22
STATEMENT OF INTENTION

I am now tuning in to the best of who I am: the part of me that is loving, giving, confident, appreciative, peaceful and patient. I open my heart and allow loving energy to flow through me. I am aware that my life makes a difference and that every action I take helps to heal the hurts within and around me.

I move into life knowing there is nothing to fear. Within me is an endless source of wisdom and strength that will handle all that needs to be handled. I am being shown the way. I move into the light and see the huge expanse of possibility. Today I push away all self-doubt and replace it with self-trust. I constantly remind myself my life is unfolding in a perfect way. I trust the Grand Design.

I am grateful for the opportunity to create love in this world. I am listening to the Divine within me. I appreciate all the opportunities this life gives me for becoming a more caring and compassionate human being. I am truly blessed.

Day 22 Affirmation

I touch the world with love wherever I go.

I commit 100% to each area of my life.
I know that I count and I act as if I do.

MY LIFE IS RICH

SPIRITUAL GROWTH
....

RELATIONSHIP
....

FAMILY
....

FRIENDS
....

PERSONAL GROWTH
....

ALONE TIME
....

CONTRIBUTION TO THE COMMUNITY
....

PLAYTIME
....

WORK

....

(OTHER)
....

RISK OF THE DAY
....

TODAY I AM GRATEFUL FOR

....

Where do I stand on my Pain-to-Power chart?

▶ ▶ ▶ ▶ ▶ ▶ ▶ ▶ ▶ ▶ ▶ ▶ ▶ ▶ ▶ ▶ ▶ ▶ ▶

PAIN   **POWER**

I am now tuning in to the best of who I am: the part of me that is loving, giving, confident, appreciative, peaceful and patient. I open my heart and allow loving energy to flow through me. I am aware that my life makes a difference and that every action I take helps to heal the hurts within and around me.

I move into life knowing there is nothing to fear. Within me is an endless source of wisdom and strength that will handle all that needs to be handled. I am being shown the way. I move into the light and see the huge expanse of possibility. Today I push away all self-doubt and replace it with self-trust. I constantly remind myself my life is unfolding in a perfect way. I trust the Grand Design.

I am grateful for the opportunity to create love in this world. I am listening to the Divine within me. I appreciate all the opportunities this life gives me for becoming a more caring and compassionate human being. I am truly blessed.

Day 23 Affirmation

I stand tall and take responsibility for my life.

I commit 100% to each area of my life.
I know that I count and I act as if I do.

MY LIFE IS RICH

SPIRITUAL GROWTH

RELATIONSHIP

FAMILY

FRIENDS

PERSONAL GROWTH

ALONE TIME

CONTRIBUTION TO THE COMMUNITY

PLAYTIME

WORK

(OTHER)

RISK OF THE DAY

TODAY I AM GRATEFUL FOR

Where do I stand on my Pain-to-Power chart?

PAIN   **POWER**

DAY 24
STATEMENT OF INTENTION

I am now tuning in to the best of who I am: the part of me that is loving, giving, confident, appreciative, peaceful and patient. I open my heart and allow loving energy to flow through me. I am aware that my life makes a difference and that every action I take helps to heal the hurts within and around me.

I move into life knowing there is nothing to fear. Within me is an endless source of wisdom and strength that will handle all that needs to be handled. I am being shown the way. I move into the light and see the huge expanse of possibility. Today I push away all self-doubt and replace it with self-trust. I constantly remind myself my life is unfolding in a perfect way. I trust the Grand Design.

I am grateful for the opportunity to create love in this world. I am listening to the Divine within me. I appreciate all the opportunities this life gives me for becoming a more caring and compassionate human being. I am truly blessed.

Day 24 Affirmation

I feel myself growing stronger and stronger.

> I commit 100% to each area of my life.
> I know that I count and I act as if I do.

MY LIFE IS RICH

SPIRITUAL GROWTH

....

RELATIONSHIP

....

FAMILY

....

FRIENDS

....

PERSONAL GROWTH

....

ALONE TIME

....

CONTRIBUTION TO THE COMMUNITY

....

PLAYTIME

....

WORK

....

....

(OTHER)

....

RISK OF THE DAY

....

TODAY I AM GRATEFUL FOR

....

Where do I stand on my Pain-to-Power chart?

▶ ▶ ▶ ▶ ▶ ▶ ▶ ▶ ▶ ▶ ▶ ▶ ▶ ▶ ▶ ▶ ▶ ▶ ▶

PAIN   **POWER**

I am now tuning in to the best of who I am: the part of me that is loving, giving, confident, appreciative, peaceful and patient. I open my heart and allow loving energy to flow through me. I am aware that my life makes a difference and that every action I take helps to heal the hurts within and around me.

I move into life knowing there is nothing to fear. Within me is an endless source of wisdom and strength that will handle all that needs to be handled. I am being shown the way. I move into the light and see the huge expanse of possibility. Today I push away all self-doubt and replace it with self-trust. I constantly remind myself my life is unfolding in a perfect way. I trust the Grand Design.

I am grateful for the opportunity to create love in this world. I am listening to the Divine within me. I appreciate all the opportunities this life gives me for becoming a more caring and compassionate human being. I am truly blessed.

Day 25 Affirmation

I say YES! to it all.

> I commit 100% to each area of my life.
> I know that I count and I act as if I do.

MY LIFE IS RICH

SPIRITUAL GROWTH

RELATIONSHIP

FAMILY

FRIENDS

PERSONAL GROWTH

ALONE TIME

CONTRIBUTION TO THE COMMUNITY

PLAYTIME

WORK

(OTHER)

RISK OF THE DAY

TODAY I AM GRATEFUL FOR

Where do I stand on my Pain-to-Power chart?

PAIN   POWER

I am now tuning in to the best of who I am: the part of me that is loving, giving, confident, appreciative, peaceful and patient. I open my heart and allow loving energy to flow through me. I am aware that my life makes a difference and that every action I take helps to heal the hurts within and around me.

I move into life knowing there is nothing to fear. Within me is an endless source of wisdom and strength that will handle all that needs to be handled. I am being shown the way. I move into the light and see the huge expanse of possibility. Today I push away all self-doubt and replace it with self-trust. I constantly remind myself my life is unfolding in a perfect way. I trust the Grand Design.

I am grateful for the opportunity to create love in this world. I am listening to the Divine within me. I appreciate all the opportunities this life gives me for becoming a more caring and compassionate human being. I am truly blessed.

Day 26 Affirmation

I allow no one to take away my good feelings today.

> I commit 100% to each area of my life.
> I know that I count and I act as if I do.

MY LIFE IS RICH

SPIRITUAL GROWTH
....

RELATIONSHIP
....

FAMILY
....

FRIENDS
....

PERSONAL GROWTH
....

ALONE TIME
....

CONTRIBUTION TO THE COMMUNITY
....

PLAYTIME
....

WORK
....

....

(OTHER)
....

RISK OF THE DAY
....

TODAY I AM GRATEFUL FOR

....

Where do I stand on my Pain-to-Power chart?

▶ ▶ ▶ ▶ ▶ ▶ ▶ ▶ ▶ ▶ ▶ ▶ ▶ ▶ ▶ ▶ ▶ ▶ ▶ ▶

PAIN   **POWER**

I am now tuning in to the best of who I am: the part of me that is loving, giving, confident, appreciative, peaceful and patient. I open my heart and allow loving energy to flow through me. I am aware that my life makes a difference and that every action I take helps to heal the hurts within and around me.

I move into life knowing there is nothing to fear. Within me is an endless source of wisdom and strength that will handle all that needs to be handled. I am being shown the way. I move into the light and see the huge expanse of possibility. Today I push away all self-doubt and replace it with self-trust. I constantly remind myself my life is unfolding in a perfect way. I trust the Grand Design.

I am grateful for the opportunity to create love in this world. I am listening to the Divine within me. I appreciate all the opportunities this life gives me for becoming a more caring and compassionate human being. I am truly blessed.

Day 27 Affirmation

I lighten up and enjoy the show!

> I commit 100% to each area of my life.
> I know that I count and I act as if I do.

MY LIFE IS RICH

SPIRITUAL GROWTH
....

RELATIONSHIP
....

FAMILY
....

FRIENDS
....

PERSONAL GROWTH
....

ALONE TIME
....

CONTRIBUTION TO THE COMMUNITY
....

PLAYTIME
....

WORK

....

(OTHER)
....

RISK OF THE DAY
....

TODAY I AM GRATEFUL FOR

....

Where do I stand on my Pain-to-Power chart?

PAIN   POWER

DAY 28
STATEMENT OF INTENTION

I am now tuning in to the best of who I am: the part of me that is loving, giving, confident, appreciative, peaceful and patient. I open my heart and allow loving energy to flow through me. I am aware that my life makes a difference and that every action I take helps to heal the hurts within and around me.

I move into life knowing there is nothing to fear. Within me is an endless source of wisdom and strength that will handle all that needs to be handled. I am being shown the way. I move into the light and see the huge expanse of possibility. Today I push away all self-doubt and replace it with self-trust. I constantly remind myself my life is unfolding in a perfect way. I trust the Grand Design.

I am grateful for the opportunity to create love in this world. I am listening to the Divine within me. I appreciate all the opportunities this life gives me for becoming a more caring and compassionate human being. I am truly blessed.

Day 28 Affirmation

I trust the wisdom that lies within me.

> I commit 100% to each area of my life.
> I know that I count and I act as if I do.

MY LIFE IS RICH

SPIRITUAL GROWTH
....

RELATIONSHIP
....

FAMILY
....

FRIENDS
....

PERSONAL GROWTH
....

ALONE TIME
....

CONTRIBUTION TO THE COMMUNITY
....

PLAYTIME
....

WORK
....

....

(OTHER)
....

RISK OF THE DAY
....

TODAY I AM GRATEFUL FOR

....

Where do I stand on my Pain-to-Power chart?

PAIN   POWER

I am now tuning in to the best of who I am: the part of me that is loving, giving, confident, appreciative, peaceful and patient. I open my heart and allow loving energy to flow through me. I am aware that my life makes a difference and that every action I take helps to heal the hurts within and around me.

I move into life knowing there is nothing to fear. Within me is an endless source of wisdom and strength that will handle all that needs to be handled. I am being shown the way. I move into the light and see the huge expanse of possibility. Today I push away all self-doubt and replace it with self-trust. I constantly remind myself my life is unfolding in a perfect way. I trust the Grand Design.

I am grateful for the opportunity to create love in this world. I am listening to the Divine within me. I appreciate all the opportunities this life gives me for becoming a more caring and compassionate human being. I am truly blessed.

Day 29 Affirmation

My life has meaning and purpose.

I commit 100% to each area of my life.
I know that I count and I act as if I do.

MY LIFE IS RICH

SPIRITUAL GROWTH

RELATIONSHIP

FAMILY

FRIENDS

PERSONAL GROWTH

ALONE TIME

CONTRIBUTION TO THE COMMUNITY

PLAYTIME

WORK

(OTHER)

RISK OF THE DAY

TODAY I AM GRATEFUL FOR

Where do I stand on my Pain-to-Power chart?

PAIN   POWER

DAY 30
STATEMENT OF INTENTION

I am now tuning in to the best of who I am: the part of me that is loving, giving, confident, appreciative, peaceful and patient. I open my heart and allow loving energy to flow through me. I am aware that my life makes a difference and that every action I take helps to heal the hurts within and around me.

I move into life knowing there is nothing to fear. Within me is an endless source of wisdom and strength that will handle all that needs to be handled. I am being shown the way. I move into the light and see the huge expanse of possibility. Today I push away all self-doubt and replace it with self-trust. I constantly remind myself my life is unfolding in a perfect way. I trust the Grand Design.

I am grateful for the opportunity to create love in this world. I am listening to the Divine within me. I appreciate all the opportunities this life gives me for becoming a more caring and compassionate human being. I am truly blessed.

Day 30 Affirmation

I embrace the world like a lover!

> I commit 100% to each area of my life.
> I know that I count and I act as if I do.

MY LIFE IS RICH

SPIRITUAL GROWTH

....

RELATIONSHIP

....

FAMILY

....

FRIENDS

....

PERSONAL GROWTH

....

ALONE TIME

....

CONTRIBUTION TO THE COMMUNITY

....

PLAYTIME

....

WORK

....

(OTHER)

....

RISK OF THE DAY

....

TODAY I AM GRATEFUL FOR

....

Where do I stand on my Pain-to-Power chart?

PAIN   POWER

I am powerful

and

I am loving

and

I have nothing to fear

much to give you have so much to give you have so much to give you have so m
give you have so much to give you have so much to give you have so much to g
u have so much to give you have so much to give you have so much to give you h
much to give you have so much to give you have so much to give you have so m
give y****
u have

ADDENDUM
Teach the Children

much to give you have so m
give y much to g
u have so much to give you have so much to give you have so much to give you h
much to give you have so much to give you have so much to give you have so m
give you have so much to give you have so much to give you have so much to g
u have so much to give you have so much to give you have so much to give you h
much to give you have so much to give you have so much to give you have so m
give you have so much to give you have so much to give you have so much to g
u have so much to give you have so much to give you have so much to give you h
much to give you have so much to give you have so much to give you have so m
give you have so much to give you have so much to give you have so much to g
u have so much to give you have so much to give you have so much to give you h
much to give you have so much to give you have so much to give you have so m
give you have so much to give you have so much to give you have so much to g
u have so much to give you have so much to give you have so much to give you h
much to give you have so much to give you have so much to give you have so m
give you have so much to give you have so much to give you have so much to g
u have so much to give you have so much to give you have so much to give you h
much to give you have so much to give you have so much to give you have so m
give you have so much to give you have so much to give you have so much to gi
u have so much to give you have so much to give you have so much to give you h
much to give you have so much to give you have so much to give you have so m
give you have so much to give you have so much to give you have so much to gi
u have so much to give you have so much to give you have so much to give you h
much to give you have so much to give you have so much to give you have so m
give you have so much to give you have so much to give you have so much to gi
u have so much to give you have so much to give you have so much to give you h

Perhaps you are thinking how wonderful it would have been if you had learned these life-affirming tools when you were very young! Well, you can't lament the past but certainly if you have children, nieces and nephews, or other children with whom you interact, it would be a wonderful gift for you to share these exercises with them. If this sounds like a good idea to you, let me give you a few suggestions:

1. The Book of Abundance is my first choice. For a child to go to bed filled with the beauty in his or her life is truly a blessing. Sharing the Book of Abundance exercise with a child is a wonderful bedtime activity.

2. Affirmations are great for children as well. It is very healing to give children Higher-Self thoughts to practise in order to replace the fear that often roams through their minds. You may want to record some affirmations with your child or buy some affirmation tapes and play them in the morning when the child is dressing, or in the evening at bedtime. (I gave one of my tapes called 'Inner Talk for Peace of Mind' as a gift to my chiropractor. He later told me that he played it for his baby over and over again and it calmed the baby greatly. He also admitted it calmed him as well!)

Once in a while, affirmation books are a great alternative to children's storybooks. It is wonderful to think of children memorizing affirmations in the same way they memorize their favourite bedtime stories. [1]

3. 'Saying Yes! to Life' is a wonderful tool for helping children find the good in all things. I would certainly buy or

borrow from the library the book *Pollyanna*, which is a classic story about positive thinking. This may seem old-fashioned to some but I feel it is truly an enlightening work for both children and adults alike.

4. Teaching children how to 'give it away' is a wonderful exercise as well. So much of children's training is about protecting what is theirs – or gaining more, more, more.

One of my favourite stories about this was told to me by one of my students. Her daughter received a huge amount of gifts one Christmas Day. After opening box after box, she finally opened the last one. Then, with disappointment in her voice, she looked at her mother and said, 'Is that all?'

Her mother was dismayed about how spoiled and insatiable her daughter seemed to be. Nothing ever seemed to be enough. Then she had an idea which made all the difference in the world. Starting in January she and her daughter began making gifts that were meant to be distributed to the children at a local hospital the following Christmas Day.

Month after month her daughter was enjoying the making of these gifts. By the time the following Christmas came along, she showed more excitement about going to the hospital and giving away her gifts than receiving the ones her mother had purchased for her. In this case, giving created magical results. What a great training for a child!

5. The 'no-complaints' game is also a wonderful exercise to do with children. In fact, a child could be your partner in pointing out your own complaining, and vice versa. You could create a game where the complainer has to give a kiss to the other. You will find yourself kissing and laughing a lot! (This is a great game to play with your mate, as well!)

6. Perhaps one of the most valuable exercises to do with children is to teach them how to 'let go of outcomes'. So many adults have too many expectations when it comes to children, especially in the areas of grades and sports. To teach a child to do their very best and then let

go of the outcome is a wonderful lesson for both parent and child.

You get the picture. Be creative. You can use all the exercises in this book to bring the messages of the Higher Self to the children who hold a special place in your heart.

You may be asking, 'What if my children are teenagers and are no longer interested in anything I want to teach them?' My answer is that teenagers may require the indirect approach. Let me tell you the story of another one of my students, Martha.

Martha came to me a as a single parent who was in a very bad way. She drank too much; she was unhappy; she felt she had no control over her life. Her teenage daughter certainly reflected her mother's state of mind. She was getting into trouble with drugs and had no focus as she went about each day.

Martha made a commitment to change herself. Without her daughter's awareness, she made the exercises I taught her a priority in her life. (In fact, she was the student I described earlier who created a rolodex of affirmations for her car.) As her Higher Self became dominant instead of her Lower Self, she changed all the patterns that made her life miserable and a happy, productive, giving and loving woman emerged.

One day her very perplexed daughter asked incredulously, 'What's happening to you? You seem so different!' Martha asked her daughter if she was interested in learning what she had learned. Her daughter said, 'YES!' and they made a game-plan. They each worked on the exercises separately during the day and reported back each night. It was a magical experience for both of them. If you met them now, you wouldn't believe they had so many problems just a few years ago. And it brought them closer together than they'd been in a very long time.

What Martha did was teach by example. It was only when *her* behaviour improved so dramatically that her daughter took an interest in learning the exercises and perhaps, as we become Higher-Self people, our children will want to follow suit – or maybe they won't.

We, too, have to learn how to let go of the outcome, even where our children are concerned. We do our best, and then let go. Remember, we all – even our children – have our own paths to follow. We have to trust that whatever path they take is for their Highest good, even if we don't understand their choices at the time. When we can 'cut the cord' in this way, we can take a deep breath and feel a greater sense of peace. How sweet it is!

ENDNOTES

Part III . . . With a Group
1. From *Dare to Connect* (Chapter 8), which gives a valuable perspective of the group process for both men and women.

Part IV
1. For more information, reach Chapter 5 in *Feel the Fear and Do It Anyway*.
2. For more practice with affirmation, read or listen to my Fear-Less series: Inner talk for a Confident Day, Inner Talk for Peace of Mind and Inner Talk for a Love That Works.
3. *End the Struggle and Dance with Life*. This talks in depth about the need for us all to enter frequently 'the Land of Tears', a very beautiful place that brings you peace.
4. For more information, read Chapter 7 of *Feel the Fear and Do It Anyway*.
5. For more information, read Chapter 11 in *Feel the Fear and Do It Anyway*.
6. For more information read Chapter 3 in *Feel the Fear and Do It Anyway*.
7. I describe my journey from pain to power in *Losing a Love, Finding a Life*.
8. Frankl, Viktor, *Man's Search for Meaning*, Beacon Press, Boston, 1963.
9. For more information about meeting and cultivating new friends read *Dare To Connect* (Chapter 7).
10. *End the Struggle and Dance With Life* is devoted to

enhancing the concept of gratitude, which I believe is the key ingredient to a joyful and abundant life.

Addendum
1. The books *Inner Talk for a Confident Day* and *Inner Talk for Peace of Mind* would work wonderfully well with children as well as adults.

ALSO AVAILABLE

FEEL THE FEAR AND DO IT ANYWAY
How to turn your fear and indecision into confidence and action
Susan Jeffers

- Public speaking
- Asserting yourself
- Making Decisions
- Intimacy
- Changing jobs
- Being alone
- Ageing
- Driving
- Losing a loved one
- Ending a relationship

Everyone has such fears throughout their lives. But whatever *your* anxieties, this worldwide bestseller will give you the insight and tools to vastly improve your ability to handle any given situation. You will learn to live your life the way you want – so you can move from a place of pain, paralysis and depression to one of power, energy and enthusiasm.

This inspiring modern classic has helped thousands turn their anger into love – and their indecision into action – with Susan Jeffers' simple but profound advice to 'feel the fear and do it anyway'.